Butler

Celebrates!

Rosie Daykin

Butter
Celebrates!

A Year of Sweet Recipes to
Share with Family and Friends

PHOTOGRAPHY BY
JANIS NICOLAY

appetite
by RANDOM HOUSE

Appetite by Random House® is a registered trademark of Random House LLC.

Library and Archives Canada Cataloguing in Publication is available upon request.

Print ISBN: 978-0-449-01686-2
e-book ISBN: 978-0-449-01687-9

Cover and book design: Kelly Hill
Cover and author photograph: Janis Nicolay
Printed and bound in China

Published in Canada by Appetite by Random House®,
a division of Random House of Canada Limited,
a Penguin Random House Company

www.penguinrandomhouse.ca

10 9 8 7 6 5 4 3 2 1

appetite
by RANDOM HOUSE

Penguin
Random
House

This book is dedicated to
Butter's wonderful customers.
Thank you for including us in
your lives and celebrations.

Contents

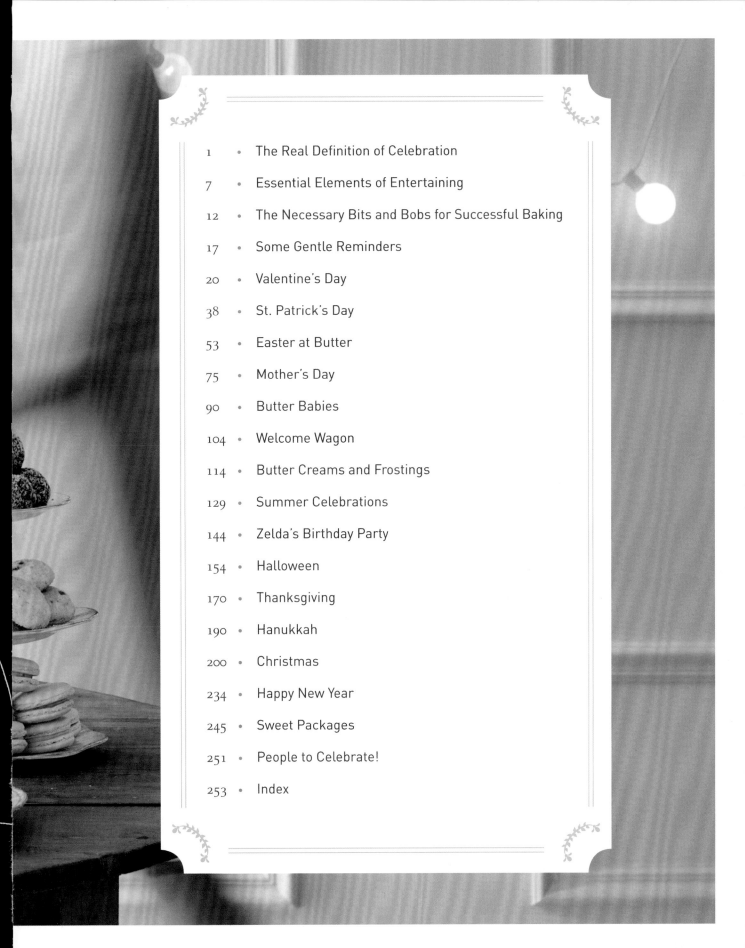

The Recipes

The Real Definition of Celebration

When I set out to write this cookbook, the first thing I did was look up the definition of the word "celebrate." It's always a good idea to get your facts straight. It read, "To observe (a day or event) with ceremonies of respect, festivity or rejoicing." Oh dear. I think I might be busy that day and have to miss the celebration because it sure doesn't sound like much fun. I mean, they didn't even mention the baked goods! What kind of celebration could it be without baked goods?

I'm not sure if *Webster's Dictionary* is still taking submissions, but, Mr. Webster, if you're out there and you read this, might I suggest that you add a little something about family, friends, laughter, love, witty toasts, good music, general chaos and delicious food? Oh, and baked goods, lots and lots of baked goods.

When I really break down the idea of a celebration, I think it is about so much more than just a date on the calendar. To me it is like a little holiday from day-to-day life. Imagine we're traveling on a train and, like life, that train is moving fast. But every so often something wonderful happens, the whistle blows and the train has to stop. It pulls into the station and lets us all off. Maybe the station is called Halloween or Mother's Day or First Day of Summer.

It doesn't matter. We've got time to explore. The next train won't be by for at least 24 hours.

I know many holidays and special events can be stressful as we wade our way through the madness of life, but there's that moment when we gather, whether we are a group or a pair, that all the duties and expectations of daily life fall away. Who cares about deadlines and carpools when the turkey needs to be carved? The laundry can wait until tomorrow, for today there is cake to be sliced. The train will get us back in time. For now, let's just enjoy. We may have to wait a whole year to share this moment again or we may only get the chance to share it once. This is what makes it special; this is what sets it apart.

I remember the day it really hit home for me what an important and privileged role Butter plays in so many people's lives and celebrations. The moment when I stopped and realized this thing called Butter was a little bigger than me and my mad desire to bake. It was Thanksgiving 2007. Having only opened the month prior, this was our first big holiday and I was more than a little nervous. I had barely gotten my sea legs and was just trying to keep my balance while I learned how to run a bakery. Thanksgiving weekend was fast approaching and the pumpkin pie orders were piling up. I stayed up most of the night, determined to get the job done. I was so engrossed in my task, I couldn't think beyond the moment those pies would leave the shop. As the day rolled on and our customers arrived to pick up their orders, I had an epiphany. A pumpkin pie epiphany. The first of its kind, I'm sure. I pictured all those people having just finished a big turkey dinner but knowingly saving room for just a little dessert. I could hear the chatter, the arguments, the bad jokes and the laughter. I could see the piles of dirty dishes painted with remnants of cranberry sauce and mashed potatoes, candles burning low and just a few gravy drippings on the good tablecloth. All over the city, families would be eating pie from Butter! Suddenly I saw myself as a guest at so many tables. They took a chance on a new little bakery and invited me into their homes and for this I will always be grateful.

I like to remind everyone who works at Butter as often as I can that we aren't just making a cake, we are making someone's birthday cake or wedding cake or bar mitzvah cake. This is so much more than cake. This is someone's life and we've been included. From the chocolate cake on which we wrote the words "Will you be my girlfriend?" at the request of a sweet

young man to the cookies we make every year for Gaby the dog's birthday all the way to the marshmallows that fill so many Christmas stockings, Butter is part of memories being made.

I didn't have a visit from the Queen in mind when I wrote this book (though I bet she would love a cup of tea and a slice of Lemony Lemon Loaf) but instead I saw the moments, big or small, that help make up a life. The very celebrations that we bake for year in and year out at Butter. These are the treats you can fill your picnic basket with as you head to the beach to watch the fireworks. It's cookies for your secret Valentine, the cake that reveals that you're having a girl or simply the fuel warm Hot Cross Buns provide before the big Easter egg hunt.

This book isn't filled with recipes but rather what I hope will become anticipated traditions. Little bits of Butter sprinkled throughout your holidays, birthdays and milestones. Even if you find just one thing among all of this that joins your list of favorites for ever and ever, I will be thrilled. It means Butter and I are going to get invited back to your house again next year and the year after that and the year after that.

For now, let's string some twinkle lights, set the table, turn up the music and make dessert. There is a celebration to be had and we'd better hurry. I think I just heard the conductor yell, "All aboard!"

Rosie

SUN MON TUE WED THU FRI SAT

Set table 1. Iron linens ✓

2. arrange flowers ✓

3. seating plan

Warm Osso Bucco

✓ Prepare polenta

Green beans 1. blanch ✓

2. zest lemon

3. pan fry

Salad 1. wash lettuce ✓

2. Toast pecans ✓

3. prepare dressing ✓

4. Assemble/dress

Assemble dessert platter ✓

Essential Elements of Entertaining

I love to entertain. That's my happy place. Standing in my kitchen dressed in my PJs, hair pulled back, music blaring, baking up a storm. I've been doing it for a long time. Paul and I celebrated twenty-six years of marriage this past August and I couldn't count how many get-togethers we've hosted, from countless Christmas dinners for twenty to summer barbeques for fifty, right down to a quiet New Year's for two. Big or small, the ingredients for a successful celebration are the same: delicious food, great people, music, laughs and baked goods. What more could you want? Having said that, there are some essential elements that I like to consider when hosting to help take the stress out of it all and show my guests how happy I am they could join us.

"HEY, ARE YOU FREE?"

I believe there is no nicer way to extend an invitation than by picking up the phone and actually speaking to someone. Emails and texts do the job just fine, but doesn't it feel great when you hear someone tell you how much they'd like to see you? Even more fun, and perhaps for something special, try sending an old-school paper invite by mail. What could be better than going to the mailbox expecting nothing but bills, only to discover a kind invitation to join your friends or family in celebration? Oh yes, please! I'm already planning my outfit.

LISTS, LISTS AND MORE LISTS

I am a list maker. Lists make me happy. They organize my head and my life. If I'm not working off a list, then I must be on vacation (and let's be honest, I make lists when I'm on vacation. How else would I remember all the bakeries I want to visit?). When entertaining, I always create a master list that includes my guests and a menu. Then I create my grocery list, making sure to break it down to various stops I would have to make—grocery store, liquor store, flowers, etc. That way I can tackle some of the tasks throughout the week, which is so much easier than trying to do it all in one day. I then make a list of all the steps involved in cooking up the menu and work my way through it. I like to break my lists down so they are quite detailed. I don't just write "make salad," as there are a lot of steps that go in to making a salad. Many of those steps can be done in advance, like washing the lettuce, toasting the nuts and preparing the dressing. By the time your guests are arriving you should only have "dressing the salad" left to cross off your list. And crossing things off the list is the part that makes me happy. The more that can be prepared in advance, the better. Making dessert the night before saves you a lot of stress the day of and leaves you time to hop in the bath before the doorbell rings.

SETTING A NICE TABLE

I like to keep my table settings pretty simple. I'm not one for a lot of pattern on the table or dinnerware as I think the food and people should always be the focus. With that being said, I think nothing could be nicer than heavy linen napkins and clean white dishes. You can always switch up the color of your table linens to work with the season or theme, but a good set of white, charcoal-gray or pale green table linens should get you through pretty much any event. But don't get hung up on the idea of traditional table linens.
A full-sized paper dinner napkin is always a good option and a wide roll of brown Kraft paper down the middle of the table makes an excellent runner. The Kraft paper can also double as place cards when you use a Sharpie marker to write each guest's name above their designated place setting.
It's just one easy, fun way to create a more relaxed environment.

THE WARMTH OF THE GLOW

Candles are a really easy and inexpensive way to create a warm and inviting atmosphere. Whether it is two traditional silver candlesticks or a cluster of old jam jars filled with little tea lights set on your table, candlelight immediately transforms a space, making it feel more intimate and special. But that candlelight will be lost in a brightly lit room and you may find you need more than a few if they are your only light source. This is why I consider dimmer switches to be one of the single most effective things you can install in your home. It allows you to control the level of light and again, like candlelight, create an inviting, warm space. I make a point of subtly lowering the lights prior to my guests arriving. Not too much, just enough to soften the edges of my home and my face.

FLOWERS, MY WEAKNESS

One of my favorite parts of entertaining is filling the house with flowers. I know you shouldn't wait until you are having someone over to put flowers out, but sometimes life gets in the way. Or you have a big fat cat that insists on drinking all the water out of your flower vases. I have a wide and varied assortment of vases that I have collected over the years but I always consider the unexpected. Once washed, an old paint can filled with roses can be just as beautiful as your grandma's cut-crystal rose bowl. And I like to keep my flowers simple. No need for large mixed bouquets. A handful of hydrangea picked from your back garden (or your neighbor's when they aren't looking), a couple of little pots of basil and rosemary or even a humble cluster of daisies will help bring your table to life, adding needed color and a subtle scent. Make sure to take a good look around the yard before dashing out to the flower shop, but avoid anything with too strong a scent. Hyacinths are one of my favorite

flowers but placed in the center of the table they would quickly dominate the entire meal and give some people a nasty headache. The same could be said for scented candles. I really love the scent many candles can provide, but I am sensitive to the fact that some guests may not feel the same. It's always best to err on the side of caution in these matters if you aren't sure of your guests' preference. I find just throwing open all the windows during the day and giving the house a good wash of fresh air can be just as effective.

TUNES TO MAKE YOU SMILE

I can't imagine a day in the bakery without music. Nothing loud and jarring, always something light and fun. It sets a mood, makes people smile and creates an energy. Paul has always enjoyed being in charge of the music when we entertain and has been known to work a playlist around a menu more than once. Who wouldn't want to listen to some retro tunes sung in Italian while enjoying a bowl of pasta, or have Bing Crosby sing "White Christmas" while you nibble on a Gingerbread Guy and sip eggnog? I'm feeling festive already!

DECORATIONS AND THEMES

When I was little, I always knew it was someone's birthday when I arrived home from school and found the tissue paper bells hanging from the chandelier in the dining room. It couldn't have been simpler, but for my family that said party! I haven't changed too much over the years. I love the suggestion of a theme using subtle details. Just like those paper bells, they create little traditions that make the day memorable. It's a tiny pinecone sitting atop everyone's dinner napkin or foil-wrapped Easter eggs sprinkled across the table. It's twinkle lights (always twinkle lights!) and wee baby pumpkins. Just a wink and a nudge to remind you why this day is special.

While many people are kind enough to plate their guests' dinner and present it to them, I guess I'm not. I much prefer to serve family-style and let everyone pick and choose how much or how little they would like to eat. I love the visual feast it creates once all the platters are filled and lining the buffet. It keeps things casual and cuts down on the stress of trying to get everyone's meal to them while the food is all still hot. I always plan what serving pieces I will need to use in advance and pull them out to remind me. I like to write the name of the dish being served on a little scrap of paper and place it in the serving piece to help me visualize the layout of the buffet. Just remember to remove those little scraps of paper as you fill the platters and bowls or someone may get an added surprise in their mashed potatoes. These may seem like unnecessary steps to take, but I have found that sometimes you can feel so organized and on top of everything and then your guests arrive and you have a glass of wine (or two) and the wheels start to fall off. And maybe you forget the bread in the oven or the salad in the refrigerator. Or maybe that's just me.

REMEMBER WHAT IT'S ALL ABOUT

Sometimes in the stress and chaos of trying to host a celebration, whether it's for two or twenty, we forget why we called this meeting in the first place. Striving to make everything just so can be exhausting and stressful. It doesn't matter if your dishes don't match or the cake is a little bit lopsided. What matters is that you set a table for everyone to gather around. There are stories to share, belly laughs to be had, candles to blow out and memories to make. Your goal shouldn't be perfection, but rather connecting with family and friends, leaving you with a full tummy and a contented smile on your face when you climb into bed that night.

The Necessary Bits and Bobs for Successful Baking

I generally try to keep my gadgets to a minimum, but there are definitely some that a good baker just can't live without. I have compiled a series of lists (more lists!) covering all sorts of things from ingredients to tools that are a good idea to have on hand should you wish to create some or all of the goodies in this book. You don't need to rush out and purchase all these items, but the lists will serve as a guide for you as you build your kitchen over time.

PANTRY ITEMS

I have tried my best to compile a comprehensive list of all the basic ingredients that make up a baker's pantry. While it doesn't cover every possible option, a cupboard filled with these items will give you an excellent start.

CUPBOARD STAPLES

- All-purpose flour

- Pastry flour (Sometimes labeled cake and pastry flour.)

- Self-rising pastry flour

- Almond flour or meal (A little costly but so worth it if you're making your own macarons.)

- Baking soda

- Baking powder

- Salt (I use kosher salt.)

- Sea salt (I use Maldon . . . lovely salty flakes for sprinkling on caramels and cookies.)

- Granulated sugar

- Dark brown sugar (Demerara is my first choice.)

- Light brown or golden sugar

- Icing (confectioner's) sugar

- Coarse sanding sugar

- Custard powder (You will want this for Nanaimo Bar Cupcakes . . . trust me.)

- Dark cocoa (Dutch-process Bensdorp, if you can find it.)

- Dark chocolate chips (Go for broke on this one because good chocolate really makes a difference.)

- Graham crumbs and chocolate crumbs (Buy them by the box already ground, it saves so much time!)

- Large-flake oats

- Spices (Cinnamon, nutmeg, cloves, ginger and anise seeds are a good start.)

- Coconut (Unsweetened medium shredded and sweetened fancy, both desiccated.)

- Nuts (Pecans, walnuts and hazelnuts, also known as filberts, will cover you for pretty much anything, but pistachios are my personal favorite.)

- Peanut butter (Love my Skippy.)

- Maple syrup (Pure, please.)

- Molasses (I always opt for fancy because "blackstrap" sounds mean.)

- Sweetened condensed milk (Can't live without it . . . not to be confused with evaporated milk.)

- Pure vanilla (As necessary as the air we breathe.)

- Alcohol (It's a good idea to have a little whiskey and brandy on hand for some of these recipes, or just for a bad day.)

- Butter, salted or unsalted (Can you ever have enough on hand? I stash a few pounds in the freezer as well.)

- Eggs

- Milk (Whole is best for baking.)

- Buttermilk (Provides a delicious tang like no other. Again, full fat is my preference, and no milk and vinegar or lemon juice substitutions!)

- Heavy (whipping) cream (33% milk fat . . . oh yeah.)

- Cream cheese (Full fat, not the spreadable kind . . . very important distinction.)

- Sour cream (Again . . . full fat. If I wanted air and water in things, I would add them.)

- Vegetable oil

- Jam (You might think about making a batch in the summer to use all year long.)

- Fresh ginger (Just a little piece goes a long way.)

- Lemons (I always have a basket of lemons in the refrigerator; try to keep at least a few on hand.)

- Fruit (Fresh is lovely when in season, but frozen works just as well through the colder months.)

The most important thing to remember when buying kitchen tools and equipment is that quality really does pay off. You might think you are saving a bundle when you buy a pair of kitchen scissors from the dollar store but they will dull after a couple of cuts (and dull knives and scissors are a greater danger than sharp ones!). Given the quality, they don't warrant the cost or effort of having them sharpened. It's better to spend a bit more on a good pair and you will have them for a lifetime. This can be said for most of the items on this list. Save the dollar store for wooden skewers, paper muffin liners and stacks of tea towels—the kind of items we would need to replace regularly.

• Measuring cups and spoons (A good quality metal set does the trick.)

• Glass or Pyrex measuring cups (A 4-cup and 1-cup measure will cover all your needs.)

• Ice cream scoops (Small, medium and large scoops are important to have on hand for all kinds of tasks.)

• Stand mixer (A bit of an investment, but you will have it for a lifetime of baking.)

• Mixing bowls (A simple set of graduated bowls. I prefer ceramic or metal.)

• Whisks and wooden spoons (You won't get far without these.)

• Spatulas (Can't have enough of these. I like the heatproof ones so there is no fear of it melting as you stir a pot of hot caramel.)

• Knives (Quality is key. Buy the best you can afford and you won't have to buy them again. A large chef's knife, a small paring knife and a large serrated knife will keep you in good stead.)

• Microplane grater (Fabulous for zesting citrus fruit.)

• Scissors (One good pair for the kitchen, get another for the craft drawer.)

❦

• 11- x 17-inch rimmed cookie sheets*

• 12-cup muffin pans*

• 8-inch circular cake pans*

• 7-inch springform pan

• 5- or 6-inch cake pan (3-inch deep)

• 9- x 13-inch rectangular baking pan

• 9- x 9-inch square baking pan

• 9-inch tube pan

• 6-cup Bundt pan

• 8-inch loaf pans*

• 9-inch glass pie dishes*

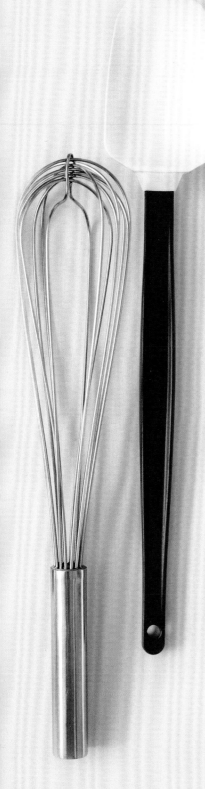

• 9-inch tart pan with removable bottom

Panettone pan (Available through most baking shops or online.)

• Wire cooling racks*

Rotating cake stand (Seems indulgent but makes the job of icing a cake so much easier.)

• Piping bags and tips (A 14-inch bag and a 10-inch bag fitted with a plain tip, star tip or petal tip will cover all your bases.)

• Pastry brush

• Variety of cookie cutters (This is a collection that can be gathered over time so try to buy nice copper ones if the opportunity presents itself, as you can have them for a lifetime.)

• A set of graduated circular cutters (Indispensable!)

• A circular doughnut cutter (Of course, a large and a small from the graduated set suggested above would work just as nicely.)

• Rolling pin (Nice and heavy, classic wood or silicone-coated.)

• Pastry blender (Brilliant little tool that has been around since time began.)

• Double boiler (You can also use a small heatproof bowl set over simmering water.)

• Parchment paper (I love parchment paper!!)

• Sieve (Great for straining but just as good for sifting all your dry ingredients. You may want to buy a smaller size as well for dusting icing sugar atop certain baked goods.)

• Plastic bench scrapers (Handy-dandy for scraping a bowl, spreading batter across a pan or cleaning up a counter of pastry bits.)

• Candy thermometer (Another of my favorite things.)

• Timers (Where the heck would we be without timers? Surrounded by a bunch of burnt baking, that's where.)

• Paper muffin liners

• Wooden skewers (The quickest way to check if your goodies are done.)

• Small kitchen blowtorch (The perfect tool for browning your meringue and toasting your marshmallow.)

• Deep-fryer (My latest investment, which I know seems crazy, but once you taste a warm jelly doughnut you may change your mind.)

*Two of each of these items would be ideal.

Some Gentle Reminders

You might think me a nag, but I feel it is important to remind you of few important tips and tricks for when you head into the kitchen to bake.

1. Always read through a recipe from start to finish before you begin. Maybe twice, just to make sure. This is the best way to avoid any surprises and to be sure you have all the necessary ingredients and tools on hand.

2. Substitutions are a fun way of making something your own, but be prepared for varied results. Swapping out the required pastry flour for whole wheat may seem like a healthier option but the end product will be completely different to the one in the original recipe. And maybe not in a good way.

3. The recipes in this book are measured using volume rather than weight as I have found it just as efficient and effective when baking in small scale. At Butter, we scale all recipes by weight because of the large volume we are working with.

4. Creaming the butter and sugar will always take a little longer than you think it should. You are looking for the butter and sugar to go from yellow and grainy to very pale and fluffy. This is best achieved by starting with butter at room temperature and being patient.

5. A good way to test if your butter is at the right temperature is by pressing on it with your finger. If the butter is too firm to leave an impression then it is too cold. If your finger slides right through the butter, then it is too warm. A gentle push should leave an indent.

6. Don't forget to scrape down the sides of the bowl throughout the mixing process. This means getting right to the bottom of the bowl so no sugar and butter get left behind.

7. When a recipe calls for melted butter I suggest that you melt first and then measure. If you measure and then melt, some of that butter will no doubt get left behind in the pot or bowl and we don't want to leave any butter behind, now do we?

8. Gently folding something in is not the same as stirring. You are trying to maintain as much air as possible to create volume and structure in your baking. Use your rubber spatula to cut through the middle of the batter, scrape the bottom of the bowl as you go and gently turn the batter over on itself to start to fold the new ingredient in. Turn the bowl slightly and repeat.

9. When whipping up your egg whites to make Mile-High Meringue Cake (page 61), for example, make sure to whip them on high speed just until stiff, glossy and smooth. Much longer and they will turn grainy and dull. A simple test is to insert your rubber spatula into the egg whites and pull it out quickly. Hopefully your egg whites will be stiff enough to hold a peak on the end of the spatula. Of course, none of this will happen if you get even a trace of fat in the bowl. So make sure to give your bowl and whisk attachment a good wipe before you begin and be careful not to get any egg yolk in the mix when separating the eggs.

10. Preheating your oven is an important step as you want to be ready to go once the batter is in the pan. It's a good idea to check the accuracy of your oven temperature once in a while with a secondary thermometer. Ovens that are running too high will bake the outside of your cakes and cookies before the insides are done, resulting in a crusty exterior. An oven that runs too low will melt your batter before it bakes, making the end product tough.

11. When placing something in the oven to bake, I always choose the center rack. If you are baking several items at once you may want to rotate the pans at the halfway point. This will help ensure all the items bake evenly.

12. When a recipe asks you to butter and flour a baking pan, do just that. Lightly butter the pan on the bottom and sides. Place about 1 tablespoon of flour in the pan and tap it from side to side to evenly coat the pan and then tip out any excess flour.

13. When lining a pan with parchment paper, butter the pan first to help hold the parchment in place and further ensure nothing sticks. Cut the parchment paper to the width of the pan but long enough so that the paper extends past two facing sides of the pan by about an inch. This creates nice little handles to help lift the bars or cake from the pan once cooled.

14. When working with hot oil or sugar, please be really careful. Focus on the job at hand and don't try to multitask. A burn is a nasty thing and really takes the fun out of baked goods.

15. Most, most, most important to a Type-A kind of gal like me: clean as you go. There is a much greater chance of mistakes or accidents happening in a messy environment and it is a heck of a lot easier to clean a couple of dishes as you are working than a whole sink-full at the end of a baking bonanza. Dishwashers are a magical thing, but quite often I find it just as efficient to wash the dishes by hand as I go and then place them on a tea towel to air-dry. That way, should I need a certain measuring cup or spoon again, it's at the ready.

16. Plan accordingly so you can enjoy the process. It's not always a great idea to tackle a new recipe the night before you have to send treats to school for your child's birthday. Keep it simple and go with tried and true. Save the more challenging recipes for a day when you have time to spare and no added pressure.

Valentine's Day

Valentine's Day is always fun at Butter. We have had just the right amount of time to get over the madness of the holidays and are ready to jump back on that celebratory horse. I think one of the nicest things you can do on this day marked for love is to surprise at least one unsuspecting soul with a Valentine. Paul and India, my husband and daughter, know how much I love them, so it doesn't come as much of a surprise when I hand them a chocolate. But what about those who don't know? What about the kind old guy at the gas station who washes my windows while I wait for the tank to fill? Does he know how much he's appreciated? I bet a little bag of Little Cinnamon Heart Cookies would show him. Can you imagine the effect Valentine's Day would have if we stopped sending Valentines to those who know we love them and started sending them to those who don't?

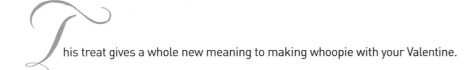

This treat gives a whole new meaning to making whoopie with your Valentine.

Chocolate Whoopie Hearts
with Raspberry Fluff Fill

2 cups all-purpose flour

½ cup dark cocoa

1 teaspoon baking powder

½ teaspoon baking soda

½ teaspoon salt

¾ cup sour cream, full fat

½ cup vegetable oil

2 large eggs

½ cup granulated sugar

½ cup light brown sugar

1 teaspoon pure vanilla

FINISHING TOUCHES
1 recipe Raspberry Fluff (page 125)

MAKES: **1 dozen (3-inch) whoopie pies**

YOU WILL NEED: **2 (11- x 17-inch) rimmed cookie sheets lined with parchment paper, 14-inch piping bag fitted with a large plain tip**

STORAGE: **The whoopie hearts will keep for up to 3 days in an airtight container.**

1. Preheat the oven to 350°F.

2. On a large piece of parchment paper, sift the flour, cocoa, baking powder, baking soda and salt. Set aside.

3. In a stand mixer fitted with a paddle attachment, combine the sour cream, oil, eggs, both sugars and vanilla. Beat to combine.

4. With the mixer running on low speed, slowly add the dry ingredients until well combined.

5. Fill your large piping bag fitted with a large plain tip with the batter.

6. Pipe twenty-four heart shapes across the two prepared trays. You could always trace the heart shapes with pencil on the underside of the parchment paper if you are too nervous to pipe them free-hand and to help guarantee a uniform size. Turn the paper over and just follow the lines to fill in the hearts.

7. Bake 10 to 12 minutes, or until the whoopie hearts are puffed and spring back when lightly touched. Remove the hearts from the oven and allow them to cool slightly on the trays before using a metal spatula to transfer them to a wire rack to cool completely.

8. While they cool, prepare a batch of Raspberry Fluff.

9. Wash and rinse your piping bag, making sure to dry it well. Refill the piping bag fitted with the same plain tip with the Raspberry Fluff.

10. Turn twelve of the hearts over and carefully pipe the filling onto each one. Top with the remaining hearts and press gently to push the filling to the outer edges.

I have never liked or understood cinnamon hearts. Nasty, spicy little things that don't taste a bit like Valentine's Day should feel. Unless, of course, you don't like your Valentine. This version, however, definitely sends a "be mine" message.

Little Cinnamon Heart Cookies

1 cup butter, room temperature

1 cup icing sugar

1 tablespoon pure vanilla

2 cups all-purpose flour

2 tablespoons ground cinnamon

1 teaspoon baking powder

1 teaspoon crushed red pepper flakes

MAKES: **8 dozen (1-inch) or 2 dozen (3-inch) heart-shaped cookies**

YOU WILL NEED: **1-inch or 3-inch heart-shaped cutter, 2 (11- x 17-inch) rimmed cookie sheets lined with parchment paper**

STORAGE: **These cookies will keep in an airtight container for up to 1 week or in the freezer for up to 3 months.**

1. Preheat the oven to 350°F.

2. In a stand mixer fitted with a paddle attachment, cream the butter and icing sugar until light and fluffy. Scrape down the sides of the bowl.

3. Add the vanilla and beat again. Scrape down the sides of the bowl.

4. Add the flour, cinnamon, baking powder and pepper flakes. With the mixer running on low speed, beat to combine.

5. On a lightly floured work surface, use a rolling pin to roll the dough to ¼ inch thick. Use your heart-shaped cutter to cut out the cookies. Carefully transfer the cookies to the prepared trays and place them about ½ inch apart.

6. Bake for 8 to 10 minutes, or until they are a light golden brown around the edges.

7. Remove the hearts from the oven and transfer them to a wire rack to cool completely.

*T*hese cookies came about at the bakery after constant daily requests from customers. I am not sure why I resisted for so long given my love for all things raspberry and almond, but when I did eventually answer the cry, I made a lot of people very happy. For Valentine's Day we cut them into pretty scalloped hearts but you can make them year-round using a simple circular cutter.

Empire Cookies

¾ cup butter, room temperature

1 cup icing sugar

1 large egg

1 egg yolk

1 teaspoon pure vanilla

2 ¾ cups pastry flour

½ teaspoon salt

FINISHING TOUCHES

1 cup icing sugar

2 tablespoons hot water

1 teaspoon almond extract

¾ cup raspberry jam

MAKES: 1 ½ dozen (2.5- x 2.75-inch) heart-shaped sandwich cookies

YOU WILL NEED: heart-shaped or 2.5-inch circular cookie cutter (plus a wee one for cutting out the centers), 2 (11- x 17-inch) rimmed cookie sheets lined with parchment paper

STORAGE: These cookies will keep in an airtight container for 1 week or in the freezer for up to 3 months.

1. In a stand mixer fitted with a paddle attachment, cream the butter and icing sugar until light and fluffy. Scrape down the sides of the bowl.

2. Add the egg and the egg yolk and beat on medium speed until combined. Scrape down the sides of the bowl and add the vanilla. Beat again.

3. With the mixer running on low speed, slowly add the flour and salt until fully combined.

4. Shape the dough into a large disk and wrap it in plastic wrap. Allow the dough to chill in the refrigerator for at least 1 hour.

5. Preheat the oven to 350°F.

6. On a well-floured work surface, roll the dough out with a rolling pin until it is approximately ⅛ inch thick. You don't want the cookies too thick as you will be sandwiching two of them together. Very carefully, using a metal spatula, transfer the cookies to the prepared cookie sheets.

7. Bake for 10 to 12 minutes, or until the cookies are a light golden brown around the edges. Remove the cookies from the oven and allow them to cool slightly on the trays before transferring them to wire racks to cool completely.

8. Meanwhile, prepare the icing. In a small bowl, combine the icing sugar, hot water and almond extract. Using a whisk or spoon, stir the icing until it is smooth and glossy.

9. Using a small teaspoon, place approximately 2 teaspoons of raspberry jam on the cookies that do not have their centers cut out. Using the back of the spoon, gently spread the jam almost to the edges of the cookie.

10. Use a small offset spatula to top the other half of the cookies with the almond icing. Don't press too hard when doing this as they are delicate cookies and you don't want your tops breaking!

11. Place the iced cookies atop the raspberry-filled bottom and press gently to sandwich them together.

This is a lovely, dense chocolate cake, easy to make and even easier to eat. Large enough to share but small enough to justify your decision not to.

Chocolate Cake for Two (or Lucky You)

¾ cup all-purpose flour

½ teaspoon baking soda

½ teaspoon salt

½ cup dark chocolate chips

¼ cup brewed coffee

¼ cup butter

2 large eggs

½ cup granulated sugar

½ teaspoon pure vanilla

¼ cup buttermilk

FINISHING TOUCHES

1 recipe Chocolate Ganache
    (page 126)

1 cup chocolate sprinkles for
    encrusting the sides of cake

MAKES: 1 (5-inch) cake

YOU WILL NEED: 1 (5- x 3-inch) cake
    pan (this cake is not layered and
    requires a deeper pan), buttered
    and floured

1. Preheat the oven to 350°F.

2. On a large piece of parchment paper, sift the flour, baking soda and salt. Set aside.

3. In a double boiler over medium heat, or a heatproof bowl set over a pot of simmering water, melt the chocolate chips with the coffee and butter. Remove from the heat and set aside.

4. In a stand mixer fitted with a paddle attachment, combine the eggs, sugar and vanilla. Mix on medium speed until well combined and pale yellow.

5. Turn the mixer speed to low and add the chocolate mixture. Beat again until well combined. Scrape down the sides of the bowl.

6. With the mixer running on low speed, add the dry ingredients and buttermilk alternately (beginning and ending with the dry). Scrape down the sides of the bowl at least twice during the mixing process.

7. Carefully pour the batter into the prepared pan. Bake for 35 to 40 minutes, or until a wooden skewer inserted in the center comes out clean.

8. Remove the cake from the oven and allow it to sit in the pan for about 10 minutes before inverting it on a wire rack to cool completely. I like to turn the cake out while it is still quite warm as it gives it a nice flat top, which is what we are hoping for when it comes time to glaze it.

9. Meanwhile, prepare the Chocolate Ganache. If you find you have some leftovers once the cake has been glazed, you can always tuck the ganache in the refrigerator, where it will keep nicely for at least 1 week. Warming it up and pouring it over ice cream is a yummy, good way to use it up.

10. Place the chocolate sprinkles in a large mixing bowl.

11. Once the cake has cooled completely, place the wire rack over a large piece of parchment or a cookie sheet. This will help catch any drips of ganache, which you can scoop up and reuse.

12. If you find the top of your cake still has a slight rise in the center, you can always use a large serrated knife to trim the top of the cake flat (the trimmed bits are lovely to snack on). Regardless, I still like to glaze this cake bottom side up, meaning the bottom of the cake ends up being the top, as this ensures a perfectly flat top on the cake—which looks the best with the finished ganache.

13. Pour a good helping of the ganache in the center of the cake and use a small offset spatula to spread it to the edges. The ganache will start to run down the sides of the cake. Continue to use the spatula to coat the sides of the cake. You can do this several times to give you a nice thick coating. Tap the wire rack lightly on the counter to help the ganache settle smoothly.

14. Once the cake has been coated in ganache, lift it off the wire rack with a large metal spatula and transfer it to one of your hands (the cake is quite dense, so fear not). Hold the cake over the bowl of sprinkles and begin pressing large handfuls of the sprinkles onto the sides of the cake. Any excess sprinkles will fall back into the bowl only to be picked up and pressed again. This saves them from flying all over your kitchen floor.

15. Place the cake on your chosen cake plate or cake board and let it sit in the refrigerator for about 1 hour, or until the ganache has set.

16. Should you wish to finish the cake with a couple of butter cream roses, follow the instructions on pages 30–31.

How to Pipe a Butter Cream Rose

Butter cream roses make for the loveliest finishing touch to cakes or cupcakes and I consider them to be a signature Butter detail. The addition of a little rose and green leaf to pretty much anything we bake instantly makes it ours. It takes more than a few tries to get the hang of making them, but don't get discouraged. Like any learned skill, a little hard work and a lot practice pays off in the end.

YOU WILL NEED: 10-inch piping bag fitted with a plain tip, 10-inch piping bag fitted with a petal decorating tip (available from craft stores), a rose nail 2- x 2-inch squares of parchment paper, small cube of Styrofoam

Fill a piping bag fitted with a plain tip and a piping bag fitted with a rose tip with the butter cream of your choice.

Use the piping bag fitted with the plain tip to pipe a tiny bit of butter cream atop your rose nail.

Top with a square of parchment paper. The butter cream will act like glue and hold the paper in place.

Using the same bag, pipe a small cone of butter cream in the center of your rose nail to create the base for your rose. Set this piping bag aside. If you need to put the rose nail down at any point (to switch piping bags or answer the phone), I find a little cube of Styrofoam works wonderfully. Just stick the rose nail upright in the Styrofoam and it will hold it until you are back in business.

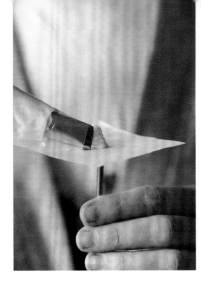 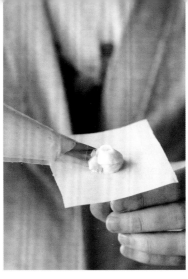 

Hold the rose nail in your left hand. Use your right hand to hold the piping bag fitted with the rose tip at a 45 degree angle, with the wide end of the tip touching the midway point of the cone of butter cream and the narrow end pointing up and slightly inward (reverse this if you are left-handed).

Squeeze the piping bag while turning the rose nail counterclockwise. Circle the cone of butter cream to create the center bud of the rose. Now you can start to create your rose petals, beginning at the center and working outward.

Holding the piping bag at a 45 degree angle while turning the rose nail counterclockwise, gently squeeze to move the bag up and down to create a small arc of icing (as though you were piping a small rainbow shape). Repeat twice to make a total of three center petals, making sure they slightly overlap. Repeat and continue to make the next layer of petals. As the rose grows, so will the number of petals on each layer.

Generally, a good rose will have about four layers: the center bud, three petals, five petals and seven petals. Slide the piece of parchment paper with the completed rose off the rose nail and carefully transfer it to a plate. Place the plate in the refrigerator for at least 15 minutes to help the butter cream firm up. This makes the roses much easier to work with when placing them. When ready to place a rose, simply use a small offset spatula or dinner knife to lift the rose off the square of parchment paper and then carefully place it atop your cake or cupcake. A small cluster of roses in varying sizes looks wonderful on the top of a cake and one single rose in the center of a cupcake is always a showstopper. At Butter, we like to finish our roses with a few butter cream leaves. Simply fill a 10-inch piping bag fitted with small leaf tip with pale green butter cream. Hold the piping bag in your right hand (or left, of course) at a 45 degree angle. Lightly touch the top of the cake where you wish to place the leaf with the tip of the icing bag. Squeeze the bag to create the base of the leaf and then gently release pressure as you pull the bag toward you to create the point of the leaf.

*W*ouldn't it be nice to surprise your Valentine with breakfast in bed? But what if Valentine's Day falls on a Wednesday and it's another chaotic morning getting everyone out the door on time and getting the dog walked and you're running late for work and the dishwasher breaks and you can't find your other shoe let alone recite a love poem to someone? That's the perfect time to slip your other half a homemade pop tart and blow them a kiss. Life's busy.

Heart-Shaped Raspberry Pop Tarts

¼ cup butter, room temperature

¼ cup cream cheese, full fat and not spreadable kind

½ cup granulated sugar

2 egg yolks

1 large egg

2 ½ cups all-purpose flour

½ teaspoon salt

FINISHING TOUCHES

1 cup raspberry jam (or your Valentine's favorite)

1 large egg

2 tablespoons water

Coarse sanding sugar

MAKES: 8 (5-inch) pop tarts

YOU WILL NEED: 5-inch heart-shaped cutter, tiny heart-shaped cutter (optional), 1 (11- x 17-inch) rimmed cookie sheet lined with parchment

STORAGE: These pop tarts will keep in an airtight container for up to 3 days but are best eaten when warm and freshly made.

1. In a stand mixer fitted with a paddle attachment, cream the butter, cream cheese and sugar until light and fluffy. Scrape down the sides of the bowl.

2. Add the egg yolks and egg one at a time, making sure to scrape down the sides of the bowl and beat well after each addition.

3. With the mixer running on low speed, slowly add the flour and salt and continue mixing until combined.

4. Shape the dough into a large disk and wrap it in plastic wrap. Refrigerate for at least 1 hour, or overnight.

5. Preheat the oven to 350°F.

6. On a lightly floured work surface, roll the dough out to about ⅛ inch thick. Cut out sixteen 5-inch heart shapes. You will need to reroll the scraps at least once. If you are using a smaller heart cutter to create a window on the pop tart, make sure to cut out the little heart on eight of the pieces of dough before you assemble the pop tarts.

7. Transfer eight pieces of the dough to the prepared tray. Use two spoons to scoop and place approximately 2 tablespoons of jam onto each heart.

8. Top each one with another piece of dough and use the tines of a fork to seal the edges of the pop tart.

9. If you have not cut little heart windows on the top of the pop tarts you will want to make a couple of slits with a knife on the top of each one to release the hot air when baking.

10. In a small bowl, combine the egg and water and beat with a fork. Use a pastry brush to coat the top of each pop tart. Sprinkle generously with the coarse sanding sugar.

11. Bake for 10 to 12 minutes, or until the jam is bubbling up and they are a lovely golden brown.

12. Remove the pop tarts from the oven and allow them to cool slightly on the pan before eating. (You don't want your Valentine to burn their lips on hot jam!!)

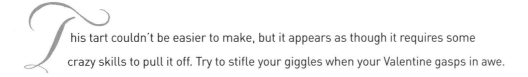

his tart couldn't be easier to make, but it appears as though it requires some crazy skills to pull it off. Try to stifle your giggles when your Valentine gasps in awe.

Lemon Tart with Raspberry Hearts

One 9-inch **Simply Tart Dough shell** (page 36)

300 mL can **condensed milk**

2 **egg yolks**

½ cup **lemon juice** (approximately 2 lemons)

Zest of 1 **lemon**

1 cup **raspberry jam**

MAKES: **1 (9-inch) tart, 8 to 10 slices**

YOU WILL NEED: **small squeeze bottle**

1. Prepare the tart shell.

2. Preheat the oven to 350°F.

3. In a large bowl, whisk together the condensed milk, egg yolks, lemon juice and lemon zest. Set aside.

4. In a small pot over medium heat, or in your microwave for 15 to 30 seconds, warm the raspberry jam until it has slightly thinned.

5. Place a strainer over a small bowl and strain the jam to remove all the seeds. Fill your plastic squeeze bottle with approximately ¼ cup of the strained jam.

6. Fill the bottom of the prepared tart shell with the balance of the jam. Use the back of a spoon to spread the jam evenly around the shell.

7. Pour the lemon filling over the jam base. Again, use the back of a spoon, or a small offset spatula, to spread the lemon fill evenly and smoothly across the tart shell.

8. Squeeze sixteen to twenty 1-inch drops of strained raspberry jam evenly around the top of the tart as if you were marking the face of a clock. Drag a wooden skewer in a continuous circle through the centers of the raspberry drops. This will create the effect of the heart border. Easy-peasy and you look brilliant!

9. Bake the tart for 20 minutes, or until it is set in the center and doesn't jiggle when you shake the pan lightly.

10. Remove the tart from the oven and allow it to cool completely in the pan.

*T*his is a very easy tart dough to make and work with. The recipe makes enough for two tart shells. Maybe instead of freezing the extra dough, you could make an extra tart and then think of someone to surprise with it. It's nice to spread the tart love all around.

Simply Tart Dough

½ cup butter, room temperature

½ cup icing sugar

4 egg yolks

1 large egg

2 ½ cups all-purpose flour

½ teaspoon salt

MAKES: 2 (9-inch) tart shells

YOU WILL NEED: 2 (9-inch) tart pans, pastry docker (or fork, if you don't have one)

STORAGE: This dough can be stored in the freezer for up to 3 months or in the refrigerator for several days.

1. Preheat the oven to 350°F.

2. In a stand mixer fitted with a paddle attachment, cream the butter and icing sugar until light and fluffy.

3. Add the egg yolks and egg one at a time, beating well after each addition. Scrape down the sides of the bowl.

4. With the mixer running on low speed, add the flour and salt. Beat to combine.

5. Divide the dough in half, shape it into disks and wrap them in plastic wrap. Chill in the refrigerator for at least 2 hours, or overnight.

6. Remove a disk of dough from the refrigerator and place it on a lightly floured work surface. Use a rolling pin to roll the dough to ¼ inch thick, adding more flour to the work surface as needed to prevent the dough from sticking.

7. Carefully fold your dough in quarters and transfer it to the tart pan. Gently unfold the dough and press it lightly into the pan. Not to worry if your dough breaks or cracks when you are transferring it. Simply position it in the pan and press gently to push it back together. This pastry is very forgiving.

8. Roll the rolling pin across the top of the tart pan to trim the tart shell and leave a nice clean edge. Roll your docker over the bottom of the shell or prick the pastry with a fork to prevent air bubbles from forming when baking.

9. Bake for 12 to 15 minutes, or until the tart shell is a nice golden brown.

10. Remove the tart shell from the oven, allow to cool slightly in the pan and then transfer to a wire rack to cool completely.

St. Patrick's Day

I remember the day I got a serious talking-down from several Irishmen via Twitter for posting an image of our cookies with the words "Happy St. Patty's Day" written atop them. Oh boy. Major screw-up. Apparently they should have read "Happy St. Paddy's Day." Am I the only person who wasn't aware of this distinction? Well, fear not, Ireland! I've learned my lesson. Happy St. Padrick's Day to one and all!

I find the making of this bread somewhat mind-boggling. How could something this easy be so darn good? It literally takes only a few minutes to pull together and before you know it, the whole house is smelling of baked bread, just waiting to be slathered with butter and honey.

Orange Raisin Soda Bread

½ cup golden raisins

⅓ cup orange juice (about half a large orange)

1 tablespoon Cointreau

3 cups all-purpose flour

1 tablespoon brown sugar

1 ½ teaspoons baking powder

1 teaspoon baking soda

1 teaspoon salt

½ teaspoon ground cinnamon

Zest of 1 orange

1 ½ cups buttermilk

MAKES: 1 loaf, 8 to 10 slices

YOU WILL NEED: 1 (11- x 17-inch) rimmed cookie sheet lined with parchment paper

STORAGE: This bread will keep tightly wrapped for 4 to 5 days. It also makes for lovely toast!

1. Preheat the oven to 425°F.

2. In a small pot over medium heat, combine the raisins, orange juice and Cointreau. Bring to a boil and remove from the heat. This will help the raisins absorb some of the orange juice and plump them up. Set aside to cool in the pot.

3. In a stand mixer fitted with a paddle attachment, combine the flour, sugar, baking powder, baking soda, salt, cinnamon, and orange zest. Briefly beat on low speed to combine.

4. With the mixer running on low speed, add the buttermilk and raisins with the juice. Beat just until the dough comes together. Turn out the dough onto a lightly floured work surface.

5. Gently shape the dough into a large round, about 8 to 10 inches across.

6. Use a sharp knife to score the top of the loaf with a cross.

7. Bake on the prepared tray for 35 to 40 minutes, or until the loaf is a lovely golden brown and sounds hollow when you knock on the bottom.

8. Remove the loaf from the oven, transfer it to a wire rack and allow it to cool slightly before diving in.

*N*ot to be confused with French macarons (page 99), these are the chewy coconut mounds from way back when. I have made a few minor adjustments to work with all things green, but should you want to serve them in July, just omit the pistachio paste.

Pistachio Macaroons

2 egg whites

1 tablespoon granulated sugar

¼ teaspoon cream of tartar

3 cups sweetened fancy coconut

½ cup sweetened condensed milk

1 tablespoon pistachio paste

1 cup dark chocolate chips

MAKES: **1 dozen cookies**

YOU WILL NEED: **1 (11- x 17-inch) rimmed cookie sheet lined with parchment paper, medium ice cream scoop**

STORAGE: **These cookies will keep in an airtight container for about 1 week.**

Pistachio paste is one of my favorite ingredients to use in the kitchen, for I am a lover of all things pistachio. It may not be stocked on your local grocery store shelves (shame on them!) but it can be found at many online gourmet retailers. It isn't inexpensive, but once opened, it will keep in an airtight container for up to 1 month in your refrigerator.

1. In a stand mixer fitted with a whisk attachment, beat the egg whites until foamy. (See page 18.) Add the sugar and cream of tartar and beat until stiff peaks are formed.

2. Fold the coconut, condensed milk and pistachio paste into the egg whites. Place the bowl in the refrigerator for about 30 minutes to chill.

3. Preheat the oven to 325°F.

4. Using your ice cream scoop, drop twelve equal portions of dough onto the prepared cookie sheet, about 1 ½ inches apart.

5. Bake for 20 to 25 minutes, until lightly golden. Remove the cookies from the oven and allow them to cool slightly on the pan before transferring them to wire racks to cool completely.

6. In a double boiler over medium heat, or a small heatproof bowl set over simmering water, melt the chocolate chips.

7. Dip the bottom of each cookie in the chocolate and place it back on the lined cookie sheet to set. Once finished, you can place the cookie sheet in the refrigerator to help the chocolate set up.

We have also made a Nutella version of this cookie at Butter that was really popular. Simply omit the pistachio paste and fill a small piping bag fitted with a plain tip with Nutella. Push the piping bag through the bottom of each cookie and squeeze to fill with about 1 teaspoon of Nutella and then continue on through step 7.

*P*aul claims these are the best brownies I have ever made. Mind you, he'd eaten a few so it may have been the whiskey talking.

Irish Whiskey Brownies

1 cup all-purpose flour

½ cup dark cocoa

2 ½ cups dark chocolate chips

1 cup butter

2 tablespoons Irish whiskey

4 large eggs

1 ½ cups granulated sugar

½ teaspoon salt

MAKES: **16 bars**

YOU WILL NEED: **1 (9- x 9-inch) baking pan, buttered and lined with parchment paper**

STORAGE: **These brownies will keep in an airtight container for up to 1 week or in the freezer for up to 3 months.**

1. Preheat the oven to 350°F.

2. On a large piece of parchment paper, sift the flour and cocoa. Set aside.

3. In a double boiler, or a small heatproof bowl set over a pot of simmering water, melt 2 cups of the chocolate chips and the butter, and whisk to combine. Remove from the heat and allow to cool slightly before whisking in the whiskey (that's fun to say!). Set aside.

4. In a stand mixer fitted with a paddle attachment, beat the eggs, sugar and salt until very pale yellow.

5. With the mixer running on low speed, add the melted chocolate and beat to combine. Scrape down the sides of the bowl. Add the dry ingredients and beat again until well combined.

6. Remove the bowl from the mixer and fold in the remaining ½ cup chocolate chips.

7. Pour the batter into the prepared pan and bake for 25 minutes, or until the brownies are firm to the touch.

8. Remove the brownies from the oven and allow them to cool completely in the pan before cutting.

I don't drink coffee, but I could definitely be convinced to start my day with one of these. One side of my brain knows that cupcakes and whiskey is a lousy breakfast choice, but the other side is screaming, "St. Paddy's Day comes but once a year!"

Irish Coffee Cupcakes

¾ cup self-raising flour

¾ cup all-purpose flour

1 cup butter, room temperature

½ cup light brown sugar

½ cup granulated sugar

2 large eggs

2 tablespoons espresso powder, plus a little extra for sprinkling

1 tablespoon boiling water

½ cup buttermilk

FINISHING TOUCHES

1 recipe Bailey's Butter Cream (page 121)

MAKES: 1 dozen cupcakes

YOU WILL NEED: 1 muffin pan lined with paper liners, large ice cream scoop, 14-inch piping bag fitted with a large star tip

These cupcakes would also be delicious frosted with a chocolate butter cream.

1. Preheat the oven to 350°F.

2. On a large piece of parchment paper, sift the flours together. Set aside.

3. In a stand mixer fitted with a paddle attachment, cream the butter and both sugars until light and fluffy. Scrape down the sides of the bowl.

4. Add the eggs one at a time, beating well after each addition. Scrape down the sides of the bowl.

5. In a small bowl, combine the espresso powder and boiling water. Stir until the espresso powder has dissolved. Add the buttermilk and stir to combine.

6. With the mixer running on low speed, add the dry and liquid ingredients alternately, beginning and ending with the dry. Scrape down the sides of the bowl several times during this process.

7. Use your ice cream scoop to fill each paper liner about three-quarters full with batter.

8. Bake for 20 to 25 minutes, or until a wooden skewer inserted in the center of a cupcake comes out clean.

9. Remove the cupcakes from the oven and allow them to cool slightly in the pan before transferring them to a wire rack to cool completely.

10. Meanwhile, prepare the Bailey's Butter Cream.

11. Fill your large piping bag fitted with a large star tip with butter cream and pipe it over the top of each cupcake. Sprinkle with a smidge of espresso powder.

*B*eer has never been my drink of choice, but I found a way to make it more appealing: I hid it in a cake covered in butter cream and pretzels. This technique was not nearly as successful with liver and onions.

Guinness Cake with Pretzels

2 cups pastry flour

⅓ cup dark cocoa

1 teaspoon baking powder

½ teaspoon baking soda

½ teaspoon salt

¾ cup butter, room temperature

1 ¾ cups granulated sugar

4 large eggs

1 cup Guinness

FINISHING TOUCHES

1 recipe Guinness Butter Cream
   (page 122)

1 large bag (280 g) pretzel sticks,
   broken

MAKES: 1 (8-inch) four-layer cake,
   8 to 12 slices

YOU WILL NEED: 2 (8-inch) circular
   cake pans, buttered and floured,
   1 (11- x 17-inch) rimmed cookie
   sheet, cake stand, large
   serrated knife

1. Preheat the oven to 350°F.

2. On a large piece of parchment paper, sift the flour, cocoa, baking powder, baking soda and salt. Set aside.

3. In a stand mixer fitted with a paddle attachment, cream the butter and sugar on medium speed until light and fluffy. Scrape down the sides of the bowl.

4. Add the eggs one at a time, beating well after each addition. Scrape down the sides of the bowl.

5. With the mixer running on low speed, add the dry ingredients and beer alternately. Begin and end with the dry ingredients. Scrape down the sides of the bowl at least twice during the mixing process.

6. Divide the batter evenly between the two prepared pans.

7. Bake for 25 to 30 minutes, or until a wooden skewer inserted in the center of one cake comes out clean.

8. Remove the cakes from the oven and allow to cool in the pans for about 10 minutes, then invert them onto wire racks to cool completely. You may need to run a sharp knife around the edges of the pans if the cakes do not easily fall when first inverted.

9. Meanwhile, prepare the Guinness Butter Cream.

10. Transfer the cakes to a rotating cake stand or cutting board and use a large serrated knife to cut each cake in half on the horizontal to create four layers.

11. Place your first layer on your cake stand (or a serving plate). Using a large offset spatula, spread butter cream evenly across the layer. Top with the next layer and repeat the process until all the layers are frosted.

12. Use your offset spatula to evenly coat the top and sides of the cake with the butter cream. Don't worry too much about how smooth the sides are because the pretzels will cover all that up. Once the cake is iced, place the cake stand or plate on a cookie sheet to catch the falling pretzels (or your dog is going to be very happy with the bounty that hits the floor). Press large handfuls of the broken pretzels into the sides of the cake until it is fully covered. Make sure you are wearing green before you start slicing!

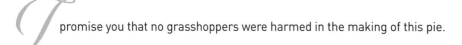

I promise you that no grasshoppers were harmed in the making of this pie.

Grasshopper Pie

½ cup butter

1 ½ cups chocolate crumbs

2 cups heavy cream

½ cup icing sugar

4 egg yolks

¼ cup granulated sugar

3 teaspoons gelatin (1 packet)

3 tablespoons crème de menthe

3 tablespoons crème de cacao

1 drop green food coloring (optional)

FINISHING TOUCHES

½ cup heavy cream

¼ cup granulated sugar

½ teaspoon pure vanilla

Mint chocolate bar, for shaving

MAKES: 1 (9-inch) pie, 8 to 12 slices

YOU WILL NEED: 1 (9-inch) tart pan, buttered, 10-inch piping bag fitted with a star tip, a large bowl filled with ice, vegetable peeler

1. Preheat the oven to 350°F.

2. In a small pot over low heat, melt the butter (or melt it in the microwave for about 30 seconds on high). Set aside.

3. In a large bowl, combine the melted butter and chocolate crumbs and stir to combine.

4. Place the chocolate crumbs in the prepared tart pan and press firmly and evenly to create the pie shell.

5. Bake for 10 minutes. Remove from the oven and set aside to cool completely.

6. In a stand mixer fitted with a whisk attachment, whip 1 ½ cups of the cream with the icing sugar on high speed until stiff. Set aside.

7. In a medium bowl, whisk the egg yolks and granulated sugar. Set aside.

8. In a double boiler or small heatproof bowl, combine the remaining ½ cup cream with the gelatin. Whisk to combine and allow it to sit for about 5 minutes to help the gelatin dissolve.

9. Place the double boiler over medium heat, or the small heatproof bowl over a pot of simmering water on medium heat, until the cream starts to boil around the edges. Remove from the heat.

10. Add a small amount of the warm cream to the egg yolks and whisk to combine. Add a bit more and whisk again. Repeat until all the cream has been added to the egg yolks. You run the risk of cooking the egg yolks and making scrambled eggs if the cream is too hot and you add it all at once. This will in turn create lumps in your finished filling. Should this happen, there's no need to panic. Just pour the cream and egg mixture through a sieve prior to chilling it in the ice bath (step 12).

11. Whisk in the crème de menthe, crème de cacao and green food coloring, if you are using it.

12. Prepare an ice bath to help cool the cream and egg mixture by filling a large bowl with ice cubes. Place the bowl with the cream over the ice and stir. As the mixture cools, it will start to thicken around the edges of the bowl. Continue to stir until it has thickened to a pudding-like consistency. Remove the bowl from the ice bath.

13. Add one-third of the whipped cream and whisk to combine. Use a rubber spatula to fold in the remaining whipped cream.

14. Fill the prepared pie shell with the filling and use a small offset spatula to spread it smoothly.

15. Place the pie in the refrigerator, uncovered, for at least 2 hours, or overnight, to set.

16. In a stand mixer fitted with a whisk attachment, combine the ½ cup cream, granulated sugar and vanilla. Whip until stiff.

17. Fill the piping bag with the whipped cream and pipe a pretty row of scallops around the edges of the pie. Run your vegetable peeler down the side of the chocolate bar while holding it over the pie to sprinkle with chocolate shavings.

Easter at Butter

*D*id I ever tell you about the year I had the brilliant idea of having the Easter bunny stop by Butter? Pure genius. I'd rent a bunny costume and fill a big basket with chocolate eggs. I imagined the squeals of delight from all our little customers when he hopped in the door. I called the costume store and arranged the rental. Then I sent out a newsletter and posted on social media about his impending arrival. This was going to be fun! At dinner that night I announced my grand plan. The conversation then went something like this:

"Who's going to wear the rabbit suit, Rosie?"

"You think it's a great idea, right, Paul?"

"Who's going to wear the rabbit suit, Rosie?"

"Well, um . . ."

"Rosie, are you honestly asking me to put on a giant rabbit costume and hand out chocolates to small children?"

Damn lawyer. Saw right through me.

*B*utter is all about delicious marshmallows and this chapter is all about Easter, so you probably saw this coming.

Coconut Marshmallow Bunnies

¾ cup water

1 envelope powdered gelatin
(approximately 1 tablespoon)

1 cup granulated sugar

¼ cup light corn syrup

½ teaspoon salt

1 tablespoon pure vanilla

2 cups unsweetened shredded
coconut

FINISHING TOUCHES

2 cups icing sugar

2 tablespoon meringue powder

Red, blue and yellow food coloring

MAKES: **1 dozen bunnies**

YOU WILL NEED: **1 (11- x 17-inch)
rimmed cookie sheet lined with
parchment paper, sharp kitchen
scissors, 14-inch piping bag
fitted with a large plain tip,
10-inch piping bag fitted with a
small plain tip**

STORAGE: **These marshmallow
bunnies will keep in an airtight
container for at least 1 week.**

1. In a stand mixer fitted with a whisk attachment, pour in ¼ cup of the water and sprinkle the powdered gelatin over top. Set aside to allow the gelatin to soften.

2. In a medium pot set over high heat, combine the sugar, corn syrup, salt and another ¼ cup water. Bring to a rolling boil and continue to boil for 1 minute without stirring. Remove from the heat.

3. With the mixer speed on low, mix the gelatin once or twice to combine with the water. Slowly add the hot sugar mixture, pouring it gently down the side of the bowl, and continue to mix on low speed.

4. Turn the mixer speed to high and continue to whip for 10 to 12 minutes, until the marshmallow batter becomes very thick, white and fluffy. Stop the mixer, add the vanilla and then whip briefly to combine.

5. Transfer the marshmallow batter to the 14-inch piping bag fitted with a large plain tip.

6. Spread the coconut in a layer across the prepared cookie sheet. Pipe twelve 3-inch long mounds of marshmallow about 2 inches apart right onto the coconut. They should be a little wider at one end than the other, just like a little bunny's body. The mounds of marshmallow will be about 1 ½ inches high. Try to work quickly as the marshmallow will start to set up in the piping bag.

7. Once you have piped all the bunny bodies, scoop up the excess coconut on the tray and sprinkle it over the tops and sides of each one. Set the tray aside for at least 1 hour at room temperature until the marshmallow sets up.

8. Once the marshmallow has set, use your scissors to create the bunny ears. To do this, make two snips in the top of the bunny, cutting in the direction of the narrower end. Use your fingers to lift the ears up off the body and sprinkle a little more coconut behind them so they stand up slightly and are no longer sticky. Repeat with the balance of the bunnies.

9. In a medium bowl, whisk together the icing sugar, meringue powder and remaining ¼ cup water. Fill the 10-inch piping bag fitted with a small plain tip with one-third of this icing. Pipe little round, white tails on the wider end of each of the bunny bodies. Set aside.

10. Return the remaining white icing to the bowl by squeezing it out of the piping bag. Add one drop of red food coloring to the bowl and stir to create a nice pale pink. Refill your piping bag with the pink icing. Give it a few squeezes to get the pink icing flowing through the tip and remove any remaining white.

11. Pipe little pink noses on the narrow end of each of the bunnies. Set aside.

12. Squeeze any remaining pink icing back into the bowl. Add one more drop of red and two drops of yellow food coloring and stir to combine. This should give you orange, and from there you can add a drop or two of blue which will create the brown icing for the bunny eyes. You can adjust the amounts of food coloring you use to create the shade you desire, but the basic combination of those colors will make a brown.

13. Fill your 10-inch piping bag once more with the brown icing and pipe two little eyes on each bunny. Allow them to sit for another 30 minutes until all the icing has set.

*T*couldn't believe what a dither I found myself in the day the Easter bunny dropped by unannounced. That is soooo like him. That big white rabbit just shows up and plants himself on my sofa expecting to be fed. Luckily, I had a batch of these cupcakes on hand, which seemed to please the big guy no end. He'd better leave me extra chocolate eggs this year.

Carrot Orange Cupcakes with Mascarpone Butter Cream

1 ½ cups all-purpose flour

1 teaspoon baking powder

1 teaspoon ground cinnamon

½ teaspoon baking soda

½ teaspoon pumpkin pie spice

½ teaspoon salt

2 cups grated carrots

¾ cup vegetable oil

1 cup granulated sugar

2 large eggs

¼ cup orange juice

Zest of 1 orange

1 teaspoon pure vanilla

½ cup unsweetened shredded coconut

FINISHING TOUCHES

1 recipe Mascarpone Butter Cream (page 120)

MAKES: **1 dozen cupcakes**

YOU WILL NEED: **1 muffin pan lined with paper liners, large ice cream scoop, 14-inch piping bag fitted with a large star tip**

1. Preheat the oven to 350°F.

2. On a large piece of parchment paper, sift the flour, baking powder, cinnamon, baking soda, pumpkin pie spice and salt. Set aside.

3. In a stand mixer fitted with a paddle attachment, combine the oil and sugar and beat on medium speed to combine. Add the eggs and continue to beat until very pale.

4. Add the orange juice, orange zest and vanilla and beat again.

5. Turn the mixer speed to low, add the dry ingredients and beat to combine.

6. Remove the bowl from the stand mixer and use a spatula to fold in the grated carrot and coconut.

7. Use the ice cream scoop to fill each paper liner about three-quarters full with batter.

8. Bake for 25 minutes, or until the cupcakes spring back when lightly touched and a wooden skewer inserted in the center of a cupcake comes out clean.

9. Remove the cupcakes from the oven and let them cool in the pan for 10 minutes before transferring them to a wire rack to cool completely.

10. Meanwhile, prepare the Mascarpone Butter Cream.

11. Fill the piping bag with the prepared frosting and pipe it over the top of each cupcake.

*B*unny Buns are a must for Easter. What could be better than the smell of warm bread, lightly scented with orange, wafting throughout the house on Easter morning? Maybe the smell of warm bread and a million bucks, but now I'm just being greedy.

Bunny Buns

1 package instant yeast

5 cups all-purpose flour

1 teaspoon salt

1 cup whole milk

¼ cup water

½ cup butter

⅓ cup granulated sugar

2 large eggs

¼ cup orange juice

Zest of 1 orange

FINISHING TOUCHES

1 large egg

1 tablespoon water

1 cup icing sugar

2 tablespoons orange juice

MAKES: 1 dozen buns

YOU WILL NEED: 2 (11- x 17-inch) rimmed cookie sheets lined with parchment paper

STORAGE: These buns are great served warm, but are just as yummy the next day with a little butter and jam. Store them in an airtight container or wrapped tightly in plastic wrap for up to 2 days.

1. In a stand mixer fitted with a dough hook or paddle attachment, place the yeast with the flour and salt. Beat on low speed for a couple of turns just to combine.

2. In a small pot over medium heat, place the milk, water, butter and sugar, and heat through just until you start to see little bubbles at the edges of the pot. Remove from the heat.

3. With the mixer running on low speed, add the warm liquid ingredients to the dry in a steady stream. Continue to beat until well combined.

4. Turn the mixer speed to medium and add the eggs one at a time, beating well after each addition. Add the orange juice and zest and continue to mix until the dough is shiny and smooth, about 5 minutes.

5. Turn the dough out onto a lightly floured work surface. Knead the dough for about 5 minutes until smooth. Add more flour to your work surface as needed to prevent the dough from sticking.

6. Lightly butter a bowl and place the dough in it. Loosely cover the bowl with a sheet of plastic wrap and place the bowl in a warm, draft-free spot. Allow the dough to rise until it has doubled in size, about 90 minutes.

7. Once the dough has fully risen, remove the plastic wrap and punch the dough down in the bowl to release the air produced by the yeast. Turn the dough out onto a lightly floured work surface and allow it to rest for about 10 minutes. ☞

8. Shape the dough into a log and cut it into twelve equal pieces. Roll each piece into an 8-inch log about 1 inch thick. Cut a 1-inch piece of dough off the end of each log and set aside. Reroll the end you cut to form a soft point.

9. Place a piece of rolled dough on a prepared cookie sheet in the shape of the letter U. Take one end of the U and twist it over and under the other end, about 2 inches up from the bottom of the U. This will create the bunny ears. Take a 1-inch piece of dough and roll it into a little ball. Place the ball in the base of the U shape to create the bunny tail. Repeat with the remaining dough.

10. Once all the bunny buns are rolled and shaped, cover the cookie sheets with plastic wrap. Set the buns in a warm, draft-free place to rise until they have doubled in size, about 1 hour.

11. Preheat the oven to 375°F.

12. In a small bowl, combine the egg and water to create an egg wash. Remove the plastic wrap from the cookie sheets and use a pastry brush to gently coat the top and sides of each bunny with the egg wash.

13. Bake for 15 to 20 minutes, or until the bunny buns are a lovely golden brown.

14. In a small bowl, combine the icing sugar and orange juice and whisk until you have a smooth glaze.

15. Remove the buns from the oven and allow them to cool slightly on the pan before transferring them to a wire rack and applying the orange glaze with a pastry brush. It's a good idea to sit the wire rack on one of the cookie sheets to catch any drips of glaze.

The big yeast question would be, what is the difference between them all? The two most commonly called for in home baking are active dry or instant. The difference between the two is that active dry yeast requires you to proof or activate it by rehydrating it in warm water before using it. The yeast has been dried and is dormant until rehydrated. Instant yeast, also known as quick-rise or rapid-rise, is composed of a smaller granule and can absorb liquid more easily, therefore not requiring to be proofed. I have chosen to use instant yeast in the recipes in this book. It allows me to add the yeast directly into the dry ingredients where the moisture in the recipe alone is enough to activate the yeast, as I have done in this recipe. In other recipes, even though it is not necessary, I have still chosen to give the instant yeast a little head start by activating it in warm water before I begin.

The combination of crispy meringue, fresh fruit and whipped cream is without a doubt one of my all-time favorite things. Traditionally this dessert is called Pavlova and is yet another yummy treat from Down Under. But in Australia it would only be one layer and pretty much nothing at Butter is only one layer. I mean, really? One layer? So this is more of a Butterlova. Three layers of fluffy meringue tinted a pale pink, just for fun, and piled high with whipped cream and strawberries. I bet you five bucks that when Australia sees this they'll start stacking things a little higher.

Mile-High Meringue Cake

MERINGUE

10 egg whites

3 cups granulated sugar

1 tablespoon lemon juice

1 teaspoon pure vanilla

3 to 5 drops red food coloring (optional)

FILLING

3 cups heavy cream

¼ cup granulated sugar

1 tablespoon pure vanilla

4 cups strawberries, stems removed, washed, dried and quartered

MAKES: 1 (8-inch) cake, 8 to 12 slices

YOU WILL NEED: 3 (11- x 17–inch) rimmed cookie sheets, 3 sheets of parchment paper large enough to line the cookie sheets, 8-inch circular cake pan, 14-inch piping bag fitted with a large plain tip, small offset spatula

1. Preheat the oven to 225°F.

2. Take the three sheets of parchment paper and use a pencil to trace the outline of an 8-inch cake pan in the center of each sheet. Turn each sheet over on a tray so the side you marked with pencil is touching the tray. The outline will show through the paper. Set the lined trays aside.

3. For the meringue, in a stand mixer fitted with a whisk attachment, beat the egg whites on high speed until soft peaks form. (See page 18.)

4. Turn the mixer speed to low and slowly add the granulated sugar 1 tablespoon at a time. Once all the sugar has been added, turn the mixer speed to high and continue to beat until your egg whites form stiff peaks, 8 to 10 minutes.

5. Turn the mixer speed to low and add the lemon juice, vanilla and red food coloring, if you are using it. Beat to combine. ☞

I have used strawberries in this recipe, but you can swap them out for all kinds of fruit, depending on the time of year. Raspberries, blueberries, blackberries, nectarines, peaches, passion fruit or a combination of all of them! You can't go wrong.

STORAGE: **This is best eaten on the day you make it. It won't go off in the refrigerator, but things will start to get a little messy and it won't look as good.**

This recipe uses a lot of egg whites. There are also several recipes in this book that call for lots of egg yolks. Store the yolks tightly covered in your refrigerator for up to 2 days and consider making some Triple Chocolate Mousse (page 241) or a batch of jelly doughnuts (page 193).

6. Fill your piping bag with approximately one-third of the meringue. Carefully pipe the meringue around the edges of the outline on one of the parchment sheets and then continue to fill in the circle with the balance of the meringue. Use your offset spatula to spread the meringue evenly across the top, creating some soft peaks and valleys as you go. Repeat for the next two layers.

7. Bake the meringue layers for 2 hours.

8. Turn the oven off and leave the trays in the oven, with the door closed, for at least 1 hour to allow them to cool completely before assembling.

9. For the filling, in a stand mixer fitted with a whisk attachment, whip the heavy cream, sugar and vanilla on high until soft peaks form.

10. Gently lift your first layer from the parchment paper and transfer it to a cake stand or plate. Don't worry about a few cracks as that only adds to the charm.

11. Use your offset spatula to spread one-third of the whipped cream across the layer of meringue. Top with one-third of the strawberries and repeat with the next two layers.

You can make the meringue layers the night before. Once they're baked, just turn off the oven and allow them to cool in the oven overnight. They will be fine in the cool oven until you are ready to assemble them. Just don't forget they are there and turn the oven back on!

*T*can get a chocolate fix pretty much any day of the year but I can only get a Hot Cross Bun fix at Easter. Unless I cheat and make them for Halloween.

Hot Cross Buns

3 ½ cups all-purpose flour

2 packages instant yeast

1 teaspoon ground cinnamon

½ teaspoon salt

½ cup vegetable oil

½ cup water

⅓ cup granulated sugar

¼ cup whole milk

3 eggs

¾ cup golden raisins

½ cup dried cranberries

½ cup candied citrus peel

Zest of 1 orange

FINISHING TOUCHES

1 egg

1 tablespoon water

1 cup icing sugar

2 tablespoons heavy cream

1 tablespoon pure vanilla

MAKES: 1 dozen lovely hot cross buns

YOU WILL NEED: 1 (9- x 13-inch) rectangular baking pan, buttered and lined with parchment paper, 10-inch piping bag fitted with a small plain tip

1. In a stand mixer fitted with a dough hook or paddle attachment, place the flour, yeast, cinnamon and salt. Run the mixer on low speed for a few turns to mix these dry ingredients together. Set aside.

2. In a bowl, whisk together the oil, water, sugar and milk. Turn the mixer speed to medium and slowly add these liquid ingredients to the flour mixture while the machine is running.

3. Add the eggs one at a time, mixing between additions, and continue to mix. Once the eggs have been fully incorporated, you can add the dried fruit, peel and zest. Continue mixing for about 5 minutes, until the dough is shiny and smooth and pulls away from the sides of the bowl.

4. Lightly butter a large bowl and place the dough in it. Loosely cover the bowl with plastic wrap and place it in a warm, draft-free place. Allow the dough to rise until it has doubled in size, about 90 minutes.

5. Once the dough has fully risen, remove the plastic wrap and punch the dough down in the bowl to release the air produced by the yeast. Turn the dough out onto a lightly floured work surface and allow it to rest for about 10 minutes.

6. Divide the dough into twelve equal pieces. Take each piece of dough and roll it loosely into a ball. Cup your hand over a ball of dough, with your fingertips touching the counter, as though you were holding a tennis ball in place on the counter. Start to roll the ball quickly around in tight circles with your hand cupped over it until you have formed a perfect little ball of dough with no seams. If you are feeling really confident, you can roll a ball under each hand at the same time, but this takes a little practice. When your arm is ready to fall off you know you are done.

7. Place the twelve balls, evenly spaced, in the prepared pan and loosely cover with plastic wrap. Place the pan in a warm, draft-free spot and allow the buns to rise until doubled in size, about 1 hour.

8. Once the buns have finished rising, remove the plastic wrap.

9. Make an egg wash by combining the egg and water in a small bowl, using a fork to whisk them until frothy. Using a pastry brush, coat the top of each bun with this egg wash.

10. Preheat the oven to 375°F.

11. Bake the buns for 20 minutes, or until they are a lovely golden brown and not sticky in the center. A wooden skewer inserted in the center should come out clean.

12. In a small bowl, combine the icing sugar, cream and vanilla and whisk until you have a smooth and glossy icing. Fill a small piping bag fitted with a plain tip with the icing. Top each bun with a cross of icing. (If there is any icing left over, people in my home have been known to split a warm hot cross bun and spread a little more across the middle, but don't repeat that.)

If you don't eat up all of these buns when they are still warm you can keep them, tightly wrapped in plastic wrap for up to 1 week. They are lovely split open and toasted.

The inspiration for this recipe came after seeing the Wes Anderson movie *The Grand Budapest Hotel*. In this movie, a very whimsical éclair, created by the fictitious bakery Mendels, played a pivotal role. I left the movie theater craving éclairs. But like all things you find inspiration in, the fun part is how you interpret them and make them your own. Or as I like to say at the bakery, how to Butter-fie it. I couldn't be prouder of this result, and I thank you, Wes Anderson, wherever you are, for your brilliant and creative mind.

Double Decker Éclairs (an ode to Wes Anderson)

1 recipe Vanilla Pastry Cream
   (page 69)

½ cup whole milk

½ cup water

½ cup butter

1 teaspoon granulated sugar

½ teaspoon salt

1 cup all-purpose flour

4 large eggs

FINISHING TOUCHES

1 recipe Vanilla Glaze (page 123)

Red, blue and green food coloring

1 recipe Vanilla Butter Cream
   (page 116)

White sprinkles (optional)

MAKES: 1 dozen two-layer éclairs

YOU WILL NEED: 1 (11- x 17-inch) rimmed cookie sheet lined with parchment paper, 14-inch piping bag, 10-inch piping bag, a large plain tip, a small plain tip, a small star tip and a leaf tip

1. Prepare the Vanilla Pastry Cream and place it in the refrigerator to cool.

2. In a medium pot, combine the milk, water, butter, sugar and salt, and bring to a boil.

3. Preheat the oven to 400°F.

4. Remove the pot from the heat, add the flour and stir to combine. Place the pot over medium-high heat and stir until the mixture pulls away from the sides and leaves a film on the bottom of the pan.

5. In a stand mixer fitted with a paddle attachment, place the warm dough. Mix on low speed for a minute or two to help cool the dough.

6. Turn the mixer speed to medium and add the eggs one at a time, mixing well after each addition. Continue to mix until a soft peak can be formed on the end of your finger when you touch the dough.

7. Fill your 14-inch piping bag fitted with a large plain tip with dough and pipe twelve 2-inch balls and twelve 1 ½-inch balls onto the prepared tray, about 1 ½ inches apart. When piping the balls, hold the piping bag vertical with the tip pointing straight down. Pipe a ball and then flick the tip away, using the edge of the piping tip to cut off the dough. This is to avoid having a little point on top of the ball, but if that seems to be proving ☞

difficult for you (it takes quite a bit of practice so don't feel discouraged, just keep making éclairs!), simply wet the end of your finger with water and press lightly on the top of each ball to remove the point.

8. Bake for 15 to 20 minutes, or until the éclairs are a lovely golden brown with a crisp shell. Remove them from the oven and transfer to wire racks to cool completely before filling and glazing.

9. Prepare the Vanilla Glaze and divide it between two bowls. Add a drop of red food coloring to one bowl to create a pale pink glaze and a drop of blue food coloring to the other to create a soft baby blue. Set aside.

10. Prepare the Vanilla Butter Cream and divide it between two bowls. Add a drop of red food coloring to one bowl to create pale pink butter cream and a drop of green to the other to create a light green butter cream for piping the leaves.

11. Fill a clean 14-inch piping bag fitted with a small plain tip with the prepared pastry cream. Pierce the bottom of each éclair shell with the pastry tip and gently squeeze the piping bag to fill the éclair. Repeat with all the éclair shells.

12. Dip half of the éclair tops in the pink glaze and the other half in the blue, allowing any excess glaze to drip off before placing them, coated side up, on a wire rack to set. You can sprinkle the smaller éclair tops with white sprinkles at this point if you are using them.

13. Fill your 10-inch piping bag fitted with a small star tip with the pink vanilla butter cream.

14. Once the glaze has set on the éclairs, pipe a small mound of pink butter cream atop each of the larger éclairs. Place a smaller éclair on top, using the butter cream to hold it in place.

15. Pipe several little rosettes on each éclair stack, spaced about ½ inch apart, at the point where the two éclairs meet. To pipe the rosettes, hold the piping bag at a 90 degree angle. Start at the center of the rosette and work outward, piping counterclockwise once around.

16. Fill a clean 10-inch piping bag fitted with a leaf tip with the green vanilla butter cream. Hold the bag at a 90 degree angle and pipe a leaf on either side of each rosette. You can tuck the piping tip slightly behind the rosette to hide the base of the leaf when you pipe.

17. Stand back and take a moment to admire your masterpiece. Okay . . . Now you can eat them.

These are best eaten the day you make them.

A good pastry cream is one of the greatest inventions out there. Right up there with tweezers and the spoon. This is absolutely heaven inside an éclair but just as delicious tucked inside a doughnut (or two).

Vanilla Pastry Cream

1 vanilla bean

2 cups whole milk

6 egg yolks

1 cup granulated sugar

½ cup pastry flour

2 tablespoons butter

1 teaspoon pure vanilla

MAKES: **2 cups pastry cream**

YOU WILL NEED: **fine mesh sieve, small paring knife**

STORAGE: **The pastry cream will keep in an airtight container in the refrigerator for up to 1 week.**

1. Using a small paring knife, split the vanilla bean down the middle. Using the tip of your knife, scrape out the vanilla seeds. Set aside. (You can save the empty pod to place in your bottle of vanilla to further enhance the flavor or tuck it inside your sugar canister to flavor your sugar with a hint of vanilla.)

2. In a small pot over medium heat, whisk together the milk, egg yolks and sugar. Sprinkle the flour across the top and whisk to combine. Turn up the heat to medium-high and continue to whisk until the mixture becomes thick like pudding, 5 to 8 minutes.

3. Remove the pot from the heat and stir in the butter, vanilla and vanilla seeds. If you don't have a vanilla bean handy you can increase the liquid vanilla to 1 tablespoon.

4. Strain the pastry cream through a fine mesh sieve into a bowl, cover with plastic wrap and place in the refrigerator to cool. If you are in a bit of a rush to cool the pastry cream, you can spread it across a rimmed cookie sheet lined with parchment paper before putting it in the refrigerator, or place the cookie sheet in the freezer for about 15 minutes to further speed up the process.

PISTACHIO PASTRY CREAM

Add 1 tablespoon pistachio paste in place of the vanilla beans and liquid vanilla in step 3.

CHOCOLATE PASTRY CREAM

Add ½ cup chocolate chips with the milk, egg yolks and sugar in step 2.

f I were a bird, this is the kind of home I would live in. But that would only be natural for us birds who like to bake.

Coconut Bird's Nest Cookies

2 cups all-purpose flour

½ teaspoon salt

¾ cup butter, room temperature

½ cup light brown sugar

1 large egg

1 teaspoon pure vanilla

1 cup sweetened fancy coconut

¼ cup raspberry jam (or jam of your choice)

MAKES: **1 dozen cookies**

YOU WILL NEED: **1 (11- x 17-inch) rimmed cookie sheet lined with parchment paper, medium ice cream scoop**

STORAGE: **These cookies will keep in an airtight container for up to 1 week or in a freezer for up to 3 months**

1. Preheat the oven to 350°F.

2. On a large piece of parchment paper, sift the flour and salt. Set aside.

3. In a stand mixer fitted with a paddle attachment, cream the butter and sugar on high speed until light and fluffy. Scrape down the sides of the bowl.

4. Turn the mixer speed to medium and add the egg and vanilla. Continue to beat until well combined. Scrape down the sides of the bowl.

5. Turn the mixer speed to low and add the dry ingredients. Continue to beat until well combined.

6. Place the coconut in a medium bowl.

7. Use your ice cream scoop to drop twelve equal-sized portions of dough onto the prepared tray. Take a ball of dough and roll it in the bowl of coconut to coat all sides. Place the ball back on the tray and repeat with the remaining dough balls.

8. Use the end of a wooden spoon or your thumb to create an indentation in the center of each cookie. Fill each indent with approximately 1 teaspoon of jam. Don't overfill them, or when the jam bakes it will bubble up over the sides of the cookie—and no bird wants to live in a messy, sticky nest.

9. Bake for 15 to 17 minutes, or until the cookies are just firm and lightly golden brown around the edges.

10. Remove the tray from the oven and transfer the cookies to wire racks to cool completely.

This cookie has it all. It's a little crispy on the outside and a little chewy in the middle and is topped with just a little lemon glaze. I'd say it's more than a little bit of all right.

Lemon Drops

2 cups all-purpose flour

½ teaspoon baking soda

½ teaspoon salt

½ cup butter, room temperature

¼ cup vegetable oil

1 cup granulated sugar

1 large egg

1 teaspoon pure vanilla

Zest of 1 lemon

FINISHING TOUCHES

1 cup icing sugar

1 to 2 tablespoons lemon juice

Zest of 1 lemon

MAKES: **1 dozen cookies**

YOU WILL NEED: **1 (11- x 17-inch) rimmed cookie sheet lined with parchment paper, medium ice cream scoop**

STORAGE: **These cookies will keep in an airtight container for up to 1 week or in the freezer for up to 3 months.**

1. Preheat the oven to 350°F.

2. On a large piece of parchment paper, sift together the flour, baking soda and salt. Set aside.

3. In a stand mixer fitted with a paddle attachment, cream the butter and oil on medium-high speed until well combined. With the mixer still running, add the sugar and continue beating until light and fluffy, about 3 minutes. Scrape down the sides of the bowl.

4. Add the egg, vanilla and lemon zest, and beat again until well combined.

5. Turn the mixer speed to low. Add the dry ingredients and beat until fully combined.

6. Use the ice cream scoop to drop twelve equal-sized portions of dough onto the prepared tray about 1 ½ inches apart. Use the palm of your hand to press down slightly on the top of each cookie.

7. Bake for 15 minutes, or until the cookies are lightly golden around the edges.

8. Remove the cookies from the oven and transfer them to wire racks to cool completely before you glaze them.

9. In a small bowl, whisk together the icing sugar and enough of the lemon juice to make a glaze thin enough to flood the top of the cookie without it running off the edges.

10. Once the cookies have cooled, use a teaspoon to place a little glaze on the middle of each cookie. Use the back of the spoon to help spread the glaze across the cookie. Sprinkle each cookie with a little lemon zest and then place them back on the wire racks for about 15 minutes to allow the glaze to set.

How is it possible that we designate only one day a year to recognize and celebrate our mothers? As the self-appointed union boss for all mothers, I move to declare any day of the week with the letter Y in it to be a day of sincere mother appreciation. Under this new proposal, all kitchens will now be closing at 6:30 p.m., all good scissors need to be returned immediately to the messy drawer and you must shut the front door to prevent heating the street. In return for these considerations, we will continue to provide shuttle-bus services, dog-walking services, costume-making services, therapy, mediation, medical attention, catering, a shoulder to cry on and unconditional love and support. Do we have a deal?

Mother's Day

*W*hen I think of my mum, I always think of tea parties. She loves them! But then, what's not to love about a tea party? Little sandwiches, baby scones, maybe a sausage roll or two. Oh, and let's not forget about the delicious cake. After all, that's what this page is all about.

Brown Butter Honey Tea Cake

1 cup butter

1 ¾ cups pastry flour

1 teaspoon baking powder

½ teaspoon salt

1 cup granulated sugar

3 large eggs

2 tablespoons liquid honey

1 teaspoon pure vanilla

FINISHING TOUCHES

1 cup icing sugar, sifted

2 tablespoons honey

Enough hot water to make a
    thick glaze, approximately
    1 tablespoon

Candied flowers (optional)

MAKES: 1 (7-inch) cake, 8 to 10 slices

YOU WILL NEED: 1 (7-inch) spring-
    form pan, buttered and floured

1. In a medium skillet over medium heat, melt the butter. It will start to foam, but this should subside after a few moments. Continue stirring the butter until you notice brown bits forming in the bottom of the pan. These are the milk solids browning, which creates a wonderful nutty aroma and taste. Remove the skillet from the heat and pour the butter into a small bowl. Place the bowl in the refrigerator for approximately 30 minutes, or until the butter has set up again.

2. Once the butter has set, preheat the oven to 350°F.

3. On a large piece of parchment paper, sift the flour, baking powder and salt. Set aside.

4. In a stand mixer fitted with a paddle attachment, cream the brown butter and sugar until light and fluffy. Scrape down the sides of the bowl.

5. Add the eggs one at a time, beating well after each addition. Scrape down the sides of the bowl several times. Add the honey and vanilla and beat again.

6. With the mixer running on low speed, slowly add the dry ingredients and continue mixing until well combined. The batter will be quite thick.

7. Place the batter in the prepared pan and use the back of a spoon or a small offset spatula to evenly spread it.

8. Bake the cake for 50 to 60 minutes, or until a wooden skewer inserted in the center of the cake comes out clean.

9. Remove the cake from the oven and allow it to cool in the pan for 10 minutes before placing it on a wire rack to cool completely.

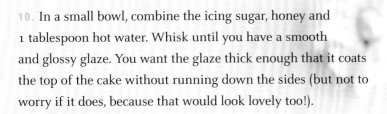

10. In a small bowl, combine the icing sugar, honey and 1 tablespoon hot water. Whisk until you have a smooth and glossy glaze. You want the glaze thick enough that it coats the top of the cake without running down the sides (but not to worry if it does, because that would look lovely too!).

11. Once the cake has cooled, use a small offset spatula to glaze the top of it and add a candied flower or two if you have them. Allow the cake to sit for about 30 minutes until the glaze has set.

*T*his is the most popular loaf we sell at the bakery. I had a lot of disappointed customers the day they discovered I didn't include this recipe in my first cookbook, *Butter Baked Goods*. I couldn't give away all my secrets right out of the gate, though, could I? If I had, this page would be blank.

Lemony Lemon Loaf

LEMON SYRUP

¼ cup lemon juice

¼ cup granulated sugar

LEMON LOAF

3 cups all-purpose flour

1 teaspoon baking powder

½ teaspoon baking soda

½ teaspoon salt

1 cup butter, room temperature

2 cups granulated sugar

4 large eggs

Zest of 2 lemons

1 cup sour cream, full fat

½ cup lemon juice

1 teaspoon pure vanilla

LEMON GLAZE

2 cups icing sugar, sifted

Enough lemon juice to make a thick glaze, approximately ¼ cup

MAKES: 2 loaves, 8 to 10 slices each

YOU WILL NEED: 2 (8-inch) loaf pans, buttered and floured

1. Preheat the oven to 350°F.

2. To make the lemon syrup, in a small pot over medium-high heat, combine the lemon juice and ¼ cup sugar. Bring the mixture to a boil and let it boil for about 1 minute. Remove from the heat and set aside.

3. For the lemon loaf, on a large piece of parchment paper, sift the flour, baking powder, baking soda and salt. Set aside.

4. In a stand mixer fitted with a paddle attachment, cream the butter and sugar until light and fluffy. Scrape down the sides of the bowl.

5. Add the eggs one at a time, beating well after each addition. Scrape down the sides of the bowl.

6. Add the lemon zest and beat again.

7. In a liquid measure cup, whisk together the sour cream, lemon juice and vanilla.

8. Turn the mixer speed to low and add the dry and liquid ingredients alternately, beginning and ending with the dry. Scrape down the sides of the bowl at least twice during the mixing process. Spoon the batter evenly into the prepared pans.

9. Bake for 50 to 60 minutes, or until a wooden skewer inserted in the center of a loaf comes out clean. The tops will have a lovely rise on them and be golden brown.

10. Remove the loaves from the oven and allow them to cool in the pans for about 5 minutes.

11. Using a long wooden skewer, poke the top of each loaf about twenty-five times. Use a pastry brush to coat the top of each loaf with the lemon syrup. When the loaves are almost cool, you can remove them from the pans and allow them to cool completely on a wire rack. Place a piece of parchment paper or a cookie sheet under the wire rack.

12. For the lemon glaze, in a medium bowl, combine the icing sugar with enough lemon juice to create a thick and glossy glaze. Spoon the glaze over the top of each loaf, allowing it to drip down the sides.

13. Allow the glaze to set for about 30 minutes before cutting.

The perfect little scone to enjoy with jam and a spot of tea. If you ask nicely, maybe Mum would share.

Lemon Thyme Scones

2 ½ cups all-purpose flour

¾ cup granulated sugar

1 ½ tablespoons baking powder

½ teaspoon salt

¾ cup butter, chilled and cut into
    1-inch cubes

Zest of 2 lemons

2 tablespoons fresh thyme leaves

1 cup whole milk

2 tablespoons lemon juice

FINISHING TOUCHES

1 large egg

2 tablespoons cold water

Coarse sanding sugar

MAKES: **1 dozen (2-inch) scones**

YOU WILL NEED: **1 (11- x 17-inch)
    rimmed cookie sheet, 2-inch
    circular cutter**

STORAGE: **These scones will keep
    in an airtight container for up to
    1 week or in the freezer for up
    to 3 months.**

1. Preheat the oven to 400°F.

2. In a stand mixer fitted with a paddle attachment, mix the flour, sugar, baking powder and salt on low speed for just a moment to combine. Add the butter cubes and mix until large crumbs form. Add the lemon zest and fresh thyme and mix again to incorporate.

3. Stir together the milk and lemon juice. Add to the dry ingredients and mix until just combined.

4. Turn the dough out onto a lightly floured work surface and roll out to about ½ inch thick. Use the circular cutter to cut out twelve circles of dough and place them on the tray about 1 ½ inches apart.

5. In a small bowl, whisk together the egg and water to create an egg wash. Use a pastry brush to gently coat the top of each scone. Sprinkle the tops with the sanding sugar.

6. Bake for 15 to 20 minutes, or until golden brown. A wooden skewer inserted in the center of a scone should come out clean.

7. Remove from the oven and allow the scones to cool on the tray slightly before serving.

y mum is great with a needle and thread. I'm better with a mixer and butter. If I could sew cookie buttons on things, maybe I'd be a better seamstress.

Orange Hazelnut Button Sandwich Cookies

1 cup hazelnuts

1 cup butter, room temperature

1 cup granulated sugar

Zest of 1 orange

2 teaspoons pure vanilla

2 cups all-purpose flour

½ teaspoon salt

ORANGE BUTTER CREAM FILLING

½ cup butter, room temperature

2 cups icing sugar, sifted

1 tablespoon heavy cream

1 teaspoon orange zest

1 teaspoon pure vanilla

MAKES: **18 sandwich cookies**

YOU WILL NEED: **food processor, 2-inch circular cutter, slightly smaller circular cutter or a champagne flute, drinking straw, 2 (11- x 17-inch) rimmed cookie sheets lined with parchment paper**

STORAGE: **These cookies will keep in an airtight container for up to 1 week or in the freezer for up to 3 months.**

1. In a food processor fitted with a metal blade, grind the hazelnuts until quite fine. Set aside.

2. In a mixer fitted with a paddle attachment, cream the butter and sugar until light and fluffy. Scrape down the sides of the bowl and add the ground hazelnuts, orange zest and vanilla. Beat again.

3. With the mixer speed on low, add the flour and salt and beat until well combined.

4. Divide the dough in half and roll each half between two large pieces of parchment to about ¼ inch thick. Place the rolled dough in the refrigerator for at least 1 hour.

5. Preheat the oven to 350°F.

6. Remove one of the dough sheets from the refrigerator and pull away the top sheet of parchment. Using your 2-inch circular cutter, cut eighteen circles of dough. Transfer the circles to a prepared tray, placing them about 1 inch apart. Repeat with the second sheet of dough so that you have thirty-six cookie shapes in total.

7. Using a smaller cutter or the top of a champagne flute, press down on twelve of the dough circles to create a button effect. Don't press too hard or you will press right through the dough. Use the straw to punch out two or four holes in the center of the circles, as you would see on a button. These are your top halves.

8. Place the cookie sheets back in the refrigerator for 15 minutes to make sure the dough is chilled prior to baking. If the dough is too warm the cookies will spread and the button holes will close up when baked.

Bake for 12 minutes, or until the cookies are a light golden brown around the edges. Remove them from the oven and carefully transfer them to wire racks to cool completely.

Meanwhile, prepare the filling. In a mixer fitted with a paddle attachment, cream the butter and icing sugar on medium speed until pale. Add the cream, orange zest and vanilla and beat again. Turn the mixer speed to high and continue to beat until the filling is light and fluffy.

When the cookies have cooled, turn the twelve bottom cookies over. Spoon approximately 1 tablespoon of filling on each and top with one of the button cookies. Press gently to spread the filling to the outer edges.

*T*am not sure why I saw this cupcake as something special for Mother's Day as I'm sure it would be pretty darn fine any old time, but given how much our mums do for us, the least we can do is let them call this cupcake their own.

Strawberry Cupcakes

¾ cup all-purpose flour

¾ cup pastry flour

1 teaspoon baking powder

½ teaspoon baking soda

½ teaspoon salt

5 or 6 strawberries

½ cup butter, room temperature

1 cup granulated sugar

2 large eggs

½ cup buttermilk

½ teaspoon pure vanilla

FINISHING TOUCHES

1 recipe Strawberry Butter Cream
   (page 117)

12 fresh strawberries

MAKES: 1 dozen cupcakes

YOU WILL NEED: 1 muffin pan lined
   with paper liners, large ice
   cream scoop, small offset
   spatula or a 14-inch piping bag
   fitted with a star tip

1. Preheat the oven to 350°F.

2. On a large piece of parchment paper, sift together both flours, the baking powder, baking soda and salt. Set aside.

3. Rinse the strawberries under cool water and pat dry with paper towel. Use a small knife to hull the strawberries and then cut them in half. Place the strawberries in a small bowl and use the back of a fork to mash them. Set aside.

4. In a stand mixer fitted with a paddle attachment, cream the butter and sugar until light and fluffy. Scrape down the sides of the bowl.

5. Add the eggs one at a time, beating well after each addition. Scape down the bowl several times during this process.

6. Add the mashed strawberry and beat again until combined. Scrape down the sides of the bowl.

7. Turn the mixer speed to low and add the dry ingredients in three parts, alternating with the liquid ingredients in two parts (beginning and ending with the dry). Scrape down the sides of the bowl several times to make sure everything is fully combined.

8. Use the ice cream scoop to fill each paper liner about three-quarters full with batter.

9. Bake for 15 to 20 minutes, or until a wooden skewer inserted in the center of a cupcake comes out clean.

10. Remove the cupcakes from the oven, allow to cool in the pan for 10 minutes and then transfer them to a wire rack to cool completely.

11. Meanwhile, prepare the Strawberry Butter Cream.

12. Fill the piping bag with the butter cream or use a small offset spatula to coat the top of each cupcake. Finish by topping each cupcake with a lovely fresh strawberry.

hiffon cake is the perfect lady cake. Or the perfect cake to eat when we are pretending to be ladies. So no foul language or crude jokes, please.

Passion Fruit Chiffon Cake

2 cups pastry flour

1 tablespoon baking powder

1 teaspoon salt

2 passion fruit

1 ½ cups granulated sugar

6 eggs, separated

½ cup vegetable oil

¼ cup water

Zest of 1 orange

1 teaspoon pure vanilla

½ teaspoon cream of tartar

Icing sugar for dusting

MAKES: 1 (9-inch) cake, 8 to 10 slices

YOU WILL NEED: 1 (9-inch) tube pan

Passion fruit is a wonderful tropical fruit that is quite fragrant. My mum is Australian, and Down Under they eat a lot of passion fruit. If your mum isn't Australian and doesn't like passion fruit, you can simply add the zest of one more orange and omit the passion fruit. Of course, then you won't have the lovely little passion fruit seeds studded throughout your cake but at least your mum will be happy.

1. Preheat the oven to 325°F.

2. On a large piece of parchment paper, sift the flour, baking powder and salt. Set aside.

3. Cut each passion fruit in half and use a small spoon to scoop out its contents into a small bowl. Set aside.

4. In a large bowl, whisk together 1 cup of the sugar, the egg yolks, oil, water, orange zest, passion fruit and vanilla. Stir in the flour, baking powder and salt until well combined. Set aside.

5. In a stand mixer fitted with a whisk attachment, beat the egg whites on high until foamy. Add the cream of tartar and continue beating until stiff peaks form. (See page 18.)

6. Turn the mixer speed to medium and slowly beat in the remaining ½ cup sugar a few tablespoons at a time. Turn the mixer speed to high and continue to beat until the egg whites are smooth and glossy, 3 to 5 minutes.

7. Gently fold the egg whites into the cake batter in three even additions, making sure not to leave any lumps as they will show up as big white spots in your finished cake.

8. Transfer the batter to the tube pan, and then use a spatula to spread it evenly around the pan.

9. Bake for 1 hour, or until the cake springs back when lightly touched and a wooden skewer inserted in the center of the cake comes out clean.

10. Remove the cake from the oven. Invert the pan. Allow the cake to cool completely under the pan before removing it.

11. Sift a little icing sugar over the top of the cooled cake. It is lovely all on its own but you can also serve it with a little whipped cream.

T am a big fan of brown sugar and I am a big fan of jam. I decided to play matchmaker with them to see what would happen. Based on the delicious results, I should probably start my own dating service.

Brown Sugar Strawberry Rhubarb Jam

1 lb. strawberries, washed, hulled and cut in quarters

1 lb. rhubarb, washed and cut into ½-inch pieces (approximately 8 stalks)

2 ½ cups dark brown sugar (approximately)

Juice of 1 lemon

MAKES: 3 (8-ounce) jars

YOU WILL NEED: 3 (8-ounce) jars, 1 (11- x 17-inch) rimmed cookie sheet, 2 large stockpots, a candy thermometer, jam jar tongs and regular tongs

STORAGE: Sealed successfully, this jam will keep in a cool dark place for up to 1 year.

1. Preheat the oven to 275°F.

2. Wash the jars with soap and water by hand or run them through a cycle in the dishwasher. Place the clean, dry jars on the tray and put them in the oven for about 15 minutes to sterilize them.

3. Bring a small pot of water to a boil and then remove it from the heat. Place the lids and rings in the water and set it aside. The hot water will sterilize the lids and help soften their wax seal. This should help give you a tighter seal on the finished jars.

4. Remove the jars from the oven and set aside.

5. In a large pot over medium-high heat, combine the strawberries, rhubarb, brown sugar and lemon juice. Cook for about 10 minutes, until the fruit begins to soften and break down.

6. Clip the candy thermometer to the side of the pot and continue cooking until the fruit mixture reaches 220°F. Remove from the heat.

7. You can check the set of your jam by taking a small spoonful and placing it on a clean saucer. When the jam has cooled, run your finger through it. There should be a pretty clean track where your finger has traveled.

8. Fill a large, deep pot with water about halfway full, remembering that when you place the jars in the water to seal them the water level will rise. Bring the pot of water to a rolling boil.

9. Using a pair of tongs, carefully remove the lids and rings from the small pot of hot water. Place them on a clean tea towel to air-dry.

10. Fill each jar almost full, leaving about ½ inch of space at the top. Make sure to wipe the lip of the jar with a clean, damp cloth as any traces of jam will prevent a good seal.

11. Screw the lids on the jars and, using a pair of jam jar tongs, place each jar in the boiling pot of water. Allow the jars to boil for 10 minutes. Turn off the heat and, using the same tongs, carefully remove each jar from the water and set them all on a clean, dry tea towel on the counter. Allow the jam to sit overnight. In the morning, check to make sure your seals are tight and secure. If for some reason one of your jars didn't seal properly, you can keep the jam in the refrigerator for at least 2 weeks.

Butter Babies

Eight years have passed since I opened my bakery, and I can't believe the pleasure I have had from watching little Butter babies grow. When we first opened our doors all those years ago, some of those babies were just wishful thinking while others were still riding shotgun in their mum's tummy. I am thrilled that Butter gets to play a part in their lives, no matter how big or how small. There is nothing more gratifying than having a three-year-old look you dead in the eye, as only a three-year-old can, and tell you how much they love your cookies. Many of those children started coming to Butter before they were old enough to chew, and today they can instruct me in glowing detail, crayon diagrams in hand, about the exact birthday cake they are hoping for. I can only hope that Butter will still be here to make them their graduation cakes and wedding cakes and, maybe if we are really lucky, way on down the road, they'll ask us to make them a Reveal Cake . . . or two.

*T*hese cookies could be any shape or size, but somehow they are best as tiny little animals with white icing and rainbow sprinkles. Perfect for little people and big people alike—and while you are munching away you can practice all your animal noises. So really, they aren't cookies at all but rather an important educational tool.

Animal Cookies

½ cup butter, room temperature

¾ cup granulated sugar

1 large egg

1 teaspoon pure vanilla

1 ¾ cups all-purpose flour

1 teaspoon baking powder

½ teaspoon ground nutmeg

½ teaspoon salt

FINISHING TOUCHES

2 cups icing sugar

2 tablespoons meringue powder

2 to 3 tablespoons water

1 cup rainbow sprinkles

MAKES: **6 dozen (1-inch) cookies or 2 dozen (3-inch) cookies**

YOU WILL NEED: **a selection of 1-inch animal-shaped cutters (or cutters of your choice), 2 (11- x 17-inch) rimmed baking sheets lined with parchment paper, small offset spatula**

STORAGE: **These cookies will keep in an airtight container for about 2 weeks.**

1. In a stand mixer fitted with a paddle attachment, cream the butter and sugar until light and fluffy. Scrape down the sides of the bowl. Add the egg and vanilla and beat again to combine. Scrape down the sides of the bowl again.

2. With the mixer running on low speed, add the flour, baking powder, nutmeg and salt. Beat to combine.

3. Shape the dough into a disk and wrap it in plastic wrap. Chill in the refrigerator for 1 hour, or overnight.

4. Preheat the oven to 350°F.

5. On a lightly floured work surface, use a rolling pin to roll the dough to ¼ inch thick. Make sure to flour the work surface as needed to avoid the dough sticking. Use a metal spatula to transfer the cookies to the prepared trays and place them about ½ inch apart.

6. Bake for 12 to 15 minutes, or until the cookies are a light golden brown around the edges.

7. Remove the cookies from the oven and transfer them to wire racks to cool.

8. In a small bowl, combine the icing sugar and meringue powder. Add enough water to make a thin icing that is easily spreadable, but not so thin that it runs off the cookies, and whisk until smooth.

9. Using a small offset spatula, coat the top of each cookie with a thin layer of icing and then top with a little pinch of the rainbow sprinkles. Allow the cookies to sit for about 30 minutes for the icing to set.

I came up with this idea for a wonderful little takeaway treat at a baby shower. Everyone loves a loot bag!

Little Meringue Booties

5 egg whites

½ teaspoon cream of tartar

1 ¼ cups granulated sugar

½ teaspoon pure vanilla

ICING

2 cups icing sugar

2 tablespoons meringue powder

2 tablespoons water

1 drop blue or pink food coloring

MAKES: **4 dozen little booties**

YOU WILL NEED: 2 (11- x 17-inch) rimmed cookie sheets lined with parchment paper, 14-inch piping bag fitted with a plain tip, small (8- to 10-inch) piping bag fitted with a plain tip

STORAGE: **The booties will keep in an airtight container for at least 1 week.**

You can save the yolks from this recipe and make yourself a batch of jelly doughnuts (see page 193)!

1. Preheat the oven to 225°F.

2. In a stand mixer fitted with a whisk attachment, whip the egg whites on high until foamy. (See page 18.) Add the cream of tartar and whip until soft peaks form. Turn the mixer speed to medium and slowly add the sugar, a couple of tablespoons at a time. Once all the sugar has been added, return the mixer to high speed and whip until nice and shiny stiff peaks form. I test this by sticking my spatula in the egg whites and quickly pulling it out. (Switch off the mixer first!) When I hold the spatula upright, the meringue should hold a stiff peak.

3. Once you have stiff peaks, turn the mixer to low, add the vanilla and beat to combine. Fill your 14-inch piping bag fitted with a plain tip with the meringue to pipe the booties onto the prepared trays. Hold the bag upright and pipe the foot of the bootie by squeezing down and making a fat little oval shape for the foot of the bootie. Lift the bag and pipe a smaller round shape atop the oval to create the ankle of the bootie. The meringues measure approximately 2 inches long by 1 ½ inches wide. Leave about 1 inch between them on the trays. If you make a mistake, not to worry. Just scrape up the meringue, put it back in the bag and begin again. It takes a little practice to get the hang of it.

4. Bake the meringues for 1 hour, or until the outside of the meringue is crisp. Turn the oven off and allow the meringues to stay in the oven for several hours, or overnight.

5. Prepare the icing. In a small bowl, combine the icing sugar and meringue powder. Add enough water to create an icing thick enough that it doesn't spread but is still pliable enough to pipe. It is best to start with 1 tablespoon of water and add from there to avoid adding too much water all at once.

6. Add your food coloring of choice or split the bowl of icing and prepare both colors.

7. Fill your smaller piping bag fitted with a plain tip with the icing and pipe a small bow on the top of the foot of the bootie and a little ruffle edge along the top line of the ankle. Allow the booties to sit for about 30 minutes, or until the icing has completely set.

*L*amingtons are a special treat from Australia. They can be a bit messy to assemble, but hang in there and stop muttering curse words, for nothing that has traveled that far is going to be easy. They are a really tasty and fun alternative to cake or cupcakes.

Lamingtons

1 Butter's Sponge Cake (page 101)

1 cup raspberry jam

1 cup heavy cream

3 tablespoons butter

1 teaspoon pure vanilla

4 cups icing sugar

⅔ cup dark cocoa

3 cups sweetened fancy coconut

MAKES: **12 to 16 Lamingtons**

YOU WILL NEED: **1 (11- x 17-inch) rimmed cookie sheet lined with parchment paper, large serrated knife, cake stand**

STORAGE: **The Lamingtons will keep in an airtight container for up to 1 week.**

Sweetened fancy coconut has a longer shred, which I think looks much nicer than regular desiccated coconut. It looks lovely on the Lamingtons or sitting on top of a cupcake or cake.

1. Prepare the Butter's Sponge Cake and let it cool.

2. Cut the cake in half across the shortest length of the tray.

3. Spread the raspberry jam on top of one cake half. Top with the other half of cake.

4. Carefully cut the layered cake into 12 or 16 pieces. Place the cake pieces on the prepared tray and freeze for at least 1 hour, or overnight. It is much easier to work with the cake once it is frozen given how delicate it is.

5. In a small pot, combine the cream and butter and warm over medium heat until the butter has melted. Remove from the heat and whisk in the vanilla.

6. In a medium bowl, sift together the icing sugar and cocoa. Add the warm cream mixture and whisk to combine until smooth and glossy. It will be quite thick, but you can thin it with a little more cream if you are finding it too hard to work with. Start with 1 tablespoon at a time to avoid adding too much. You don't want that icing running off the cake.

7. Fill a large bowl with the coconut.

8. Lots of people would tell you to dip the cake into the chocolate icing, coat it in icing and then roll it in the coconut. I found this to be the really messy part and not very effective. And it made me quite grumpy. Instead, using a small offset spatula, spread a small amount of the chocolate icing on the center of a cake stand (I find it easier to work with the cakes if they are elevated). Place a piece of the frozen cake atop the icing on the cake stand. The icing works a little bit like glue, holding it in

place while you ice all the other sides. Coat the sides and top of the cake and then use the spatula to lift the cake and the icing on the bottom from the cake stand. Now drop it into the bowl of coconut and roll it around to coat all sides.

9. Lift the Lamington from the coconut and place it on a clean tray or plate. Repeat with the rest of the pieces of cake. Allow the Lamingtons to sit at room temperature for about 30 minutes for the icing to set.

Dark cocoa or Dutch-processed differs from natural cocoa powder in two big ways. Dutch-process cocoa has had the acid removed from the cocoa powder and is darker in color. Natural cocoa powder has not had the acid neutralized and is much lighter in color. I prefer to use Dutch-process cocoa in my recipes, but in a pinch, if you don't have any on hand, you can use natural. Keep in mind that the end results may not be the same. Check the recipe for the leavener that is called for. Natural cocoa powder is naturally paired with baking soda as baking soda needs an acid to activate it. Dutch-process cocoa, having had its acid stripped, works better with baking powder. For optimum results, always try to make the recipe as instructed.

FIRST YEAR   A Beatrix Potter Baby Book

T don't know anyone who doesn't love macarons. Just like the French, they can be a little intimidating, but once you crack through that crisp outer shell, they are sweet as can be in the middle. There is definitely a practice effect when it comes to making these cookies. Stick with it, for once you get the hang of them, they are one of the most rewarding cookies to make.

French Macarons

1 cup almond meal

1 cup icing sugar

3 egg whites

¼ cup granulated sugar

FINISHING TOUCHES
1 recipe Vanilla Butter Cream
    (page 116)

MAKES: 1 dozen (2-inch) macarons

WHAT YOU WILL NEED: 2 (11- x 17-inch) rimmed cookie sheets, 2 (11- x 17-inch) sheets of parchment paper, 14-inch piping bag fitted with a plain tip, food processor

STORAGE: The macarons will keep in an airtight container for several days but they will also freeze beautifully, filled or unfilled, for up to 1 month.

1. On the back side of each piece of parchment paper, use a circular cutter and a pencil to trace the outline of twenty-four 2-inch circles. Mark them about 1 inch apart. Turn the papers right side up on the trays. The pencil tracings will show through the paper and act as your guide when piping the cookies.

2. In a food processor fitted with a steel blade, pulse the almond meal and icing sugar until very fine. Set aside.

3. In a stand mixer fitted with a whisk attachment, whip the egg whites on high speed until foamy. (See page 18.)

4. Gradually add the sugar 1 tablespoon at a time until stiff peaks form.

5. Fold the almond-flour mixture into the egg white in three additions. Once all the flour has been folded into the egg whites, continue folding until the macaron batter has broken down to a consistency like a thick cake batter. When you hold the spatula up, the batter should run off in thick ribbons. This is the little secret that gives you lovely smooth tops on the macarons. If you don't fold the batter long enough, it will be too stiff and your macarons too thick, leading to cracks on top. ☞

Almond meal or flour is made from whole, blanched almonds that have been finely ground. It has a grittier consistency than regular flour but offers a lovely nutty flavor and added moisture. Given that it is more costly than other flours, I reserve its use for specialty items like these French macarons.

6. Fit a plain tip on your large piping bag and fill the bag with the macaron batter. Hold the piping bag upright and pipe the batter straight down onto the prepared trays, using the circles on the parchment paper to guide you.

7. Once you have piped all the macarons, give the trays a light tap on the edge of the counter to release any air bubbles.

8. Allow the trays to sit for at least 30 minutes, or until the macarons have formed a skin on top and are dull in color. If you touch them with your finger they should not be sticky. This is a crucial step in making successful macarons.

9. Preheat the oven to 325°F.

10. Place the trays in the oven and bake the macarons for 10 to 12 minutes, or until crisp on top.

11. Remove the macarons from the oven and allow them to cool completely on the trays.

12. Wash and dry your piping bag and plain tip as you will need to reload it with butter cream.

13. Fill the piping bag with Vanilla Butter Cream (or flavor of your choice) and turn half of the macarons over so that they are flat side up. Pipe a small dollop of butter cream on the bottoms and then top with the balance of the macarons. Press the two sides together gently to help spread the butter cream to the outer edges of the cookie.

Macaron Flavor Options

VANILLA MACARONS

Add 1 teaspoon pure vanilla to the basic macaron recipe

Fill the cookies with Vanilla Butter Cream (page 116)

RASPBERRY MACARONS

Fold in 1 to 2 drops pink food coloring to the basic macaron recipe

Add 2 drops pink food coloring to Vanilla Butter Cream (page 116)

Pipe a circle of the pink butter cream on the bottom halves of the cookies
and fill the center of each circle with 1 teaspoon raspberry jam

MINT MACARONS

Add 1 to 2 drops green food coloring to the basic macaron recipe

Add 1 to 2 drops green food coloring and 1 teaspoon mint flavor to
Vanilla Butter Cream (page 116)

MOCHA MACARONS

Fold 2 tablespoons sifted dark cocoa into the basic macaron recipe

Fill with Coffee Italian Butter Cream (page 118)

A sponge cake is a wonderful thing given all the different ways you can use it. It is the base for my Lamingtons (page 96), but it would be just as delicious layered with Raspberry Fluff (page 125) and rolled into a log. Actually, that would be awesome. I'm going to make that right now. Talk soon.

Butter's Sponge Cake

1 ¼ cups pastry flour

8 large eggs, separated

1 ½ teaspoons cream of tartar

1 ¾ cups granulated sugar

1 ½ teaspoons pure vanilla

MAKES: **1 (approximately 8- x 11-inch) two-layer sheet cake**

YOU WILL NEED: **1 (11- x 17-inch) rimmed cookie sheet lined with parchment paper**

Should you choose to roll the cake, begin by first inverting the warm cake onto a clean tea towel sprinkled with granulated sugar. Remove the parchment from the bottom of the cake. Gently roll the cake up in the tea towel, starting at one of the short sides. Transfer the rolled cake in the tea towel to a wire rack to cool completely. Once cool, gently unroll the cake, spread with your desired filling, reroll and transfer to a platter or cake plate for serving.

1. Preheat the oven to 350°F.

2. On a large piece of parchment paper, sift the pastry flour. Set aside.

3. Place the egg whites in the bowl of a stand mixer fitted with a whisk attachment and beat on high until foamy. (See page 18.) Add the cream of tartar and beat again until soft peaks form. With the mixer still running, gradually add ¼ cup of the sugar and continue beating until stiff, glossy peaks form. Transfer the egg whites to a large mixing bowl.

4. Return the bowl of the mixer to the stand, with the whisk attachment still fitted, and add the egg yolks, the remaining 1 ½ cups granulated sugar and the vanilla. Beat on high speed until the yolks are a very pale yellow and have doubled in volume, 3 to 5 minutes.

5. Gently fold the egg yolks into the stiff egg whites and then fold in the pastry flour.

6. Pour the batter onto the prepared cookie sheet and use a small offset spatula to spread it evenly across the tray.

7. Bake for 13 to 15 minutes, or until the cake springs back when lightly touched.

8. Remove the cake from the oven. Allow it to cool completely in the tray before cutting and layering it.

I remember the first time a young couple expecting their first child came into Butter with what I thought was the strangest request. Would we make them a reveal cake? "A what?" I asked. They patiently explained that they were planning a party and would need a cake that was either pink or blue on the inside to indicate who was headed their way. We are game for pretty much anything at Butter, so of course I agreed. The next day, a sealed envelope was delivered from the doctor's office. Not even the proud parents were to know the answer until the cake was sliced. I have to admit, it was pretty fun for all of us to be entrusted with this little secret. It felt like our baby. Since then, we have made lots of reveal cakes. This confirms what I have always believed: cake can pretty much provide the answer to any question.

The Reveal Cake

3 ½ cups pastry flour

2 teaspoon baking powder

1 teaspoon salt

1 cup butter, room temperature

2 cups granulated sugar

¼ cup light corn syrup

4 large eggs

1 ½ cups water

2 teaspoons pure vanilla

3 to 5 drops pink or blue food
    coloring

FINISHING TOUCHES

1 recipe Vanilla Butter Cream
    (page 116)

MAKES: 1 (8-inch) four-layer cake

YOU WILL NEED: 2 (8-inch) circular
    cake pans, buttered and floured,
    large serrated knife, large offset
    spatula

1. Preheat the oven to 350°F.

2. On a large piece of parchment paper sift the flour, baking powder and salt. Set aside.

3. In a stand mixer fitted with a paddle attachment, cream the butter, sugar and corn syrup until light and fluffy. Scrape down the sides of the bowl.

4. Add the eggs, water and vanilla in one addition. Beat again. Scrape down the sides of the bowl again.

5. With the mixer running on low speed, add the dry ingredients in three stages, beating well between each addition, until combined.

6. Add the appropriate food coloring and beat again.

7. Divide the batter between the prepared pans and use a small offset spatula to spread the batter evenly across the pans.

8. Bake for 20 to 25 minutes, or until a wooden skewer inserted in the center of a cake comes out clean.

9. Remove the cakes from the oven and allow them to cool slightly in the pans before turning them out onto wire racks to cool completely. You may need to run a small knife around the edges of the pan if the cakes do not fall easily when first inverted.

10. Once the cakes have cooled, use a large serrated knife to cut each cake in half horizontally, creating four layers.

11. Prepare the Vanilla Butter Cream.

12. Place one layer of the cake on a cake stand or plate. Using a large offset spatula, spread a generous helping of butter cream evenly and smoothly across it. Top with the next layer and repeat with the remaining layers. Cover the top and sides of the cake with the remaining butter cream. You may want to apply a thin undercoat of butter cream on the cake first and then place it in the refrigerator to set up before proceeding with the final coat. We want to make sure no clue of the color peaks through and spoils the surprise!

Welcome Wagon

One of the best parts of opening Butter was becoming part of a neighborhood. I loved the process and rhythm of slowly, day by day, getting to know all our regular customers and their kids. I looked forward to chatting with our UPS guy and our mailman, our bank tellers and the family who owns the produce store. I like the feeling of comfort and security I get when I wave to Ellen at the dry cleaner's, or just simply knowing I can run up to Jessica's flower shop for a chat if I'm having a rough day. The comfort comes from making a connection, no matter how small or brief it might be, with the people who share our lives. It reminds us that we aren't alone and it helps make this big, crazy world just a little bit smaller.

*I*f I had just moved into my new home and I was up to my armpits in packing boxes and my neighbor appeared at my door carrying this loaf I'm pretty sure—no, I'm absolutely sure—we would become good friends.

Dark Chocolate Cherry Loaf

1 ⅓ cups pastry flour

¾ teaspoon baking powder

½ teaspoon salt

¾ cup butter, room temperature

¾ cup light brown sugar

3 large eggs

1 tablespoon kirsch

1 cup dark chocolate chips

½ cup dried sour cherries

MAKES: **1 (8-inch) loaf, 8 to 10 slices**

YOU WILL NEED: **1 (8-inch) loaf pan, buttered and floured**

STORAGE: **Wrapped tightly in plastic wrap or stored in an airtight container, this loaf will keep for up to 1 week, or up to 3 months in the freezer.**

1. Preheat the oven to 350°F.

2. On a large piece of parchment paper, sift the flour, baking powder and salt. Set aside.

3. In a stand mixer fitted with a paddle attachment, cream the butter and sugar on high speed until light and fluffy. Scrape down the sides of the bowl with a spatula.

4. Add the eggs one at a time, beating well after each addition. Scrape down the sides of the bowl. Add the kirsch and beat again.

5. With the mixer running on low speed, add the dry ingredients and beat until just combined. Add the chocolate chips and cherries, and beat again.

6. Pour the batter into the prepared pan and use a small offset spatula to spread it smoothly across the pan.

7. Bake for 45 to 50 minutes, or until a wooden skewer inserted in the center of the loaf comes out clean.

8. Remove the loaf from the oven and allow it to cool slightly in the pan before transferring it to a wire rack to cool completely. Use a serrated knife to slice the loaf.

I have always thought that a lovely and delicious housewarming gift is a classic glass cookie jar filled to the brim with homemade cookies. Who the heck doesn't need a cookie jar? And if you promise to refill it every time you stop by, all the better. Bet you get invited back real fast!

Cookie Jar Cookies

2 cups all-purpose flour

1 teaspoon baking soda

½ teaspoon salt

1 cup butter, room temperature

¾ cup dark brown sugar

½ cup granulated sugar

2 large eggs

1 teaspoon pure vanilla

1 cup dark chocolate chips

½ cup unsweetened shredded coconut

½ cup large-flake rolled oats

½ cup chopped pecans

MAKES: **2 dozen cookies**

YOU WILL NEED: **2 (11- x 17-inch) rimmed cookie sheets lined with parchment paper, medium ice cream scoop**

STORAGE: **These cookies will keep in an airtight container for up to 1 week or in the freezer for up to 3 months.**

1. Preheat the oven to 350°F.

2. On a large piece of parchment paper, sift the flour, baking soda and salt. Set aside.

3. In a stand mixer fitted with a paddle attachment, cream the butter and both sugars on high speed until light and fluffy. Scrape down the sides of the bowl.

4. Add the eggs one at a time, beating briefly after each addition. Scrape down the sides of the bowl. Add the vanilla and beat again.

5. Turn the mixer speed to low and add the dry ingredients. Beat to combine.

6. Add the chocolate chips, coconut, oats and pecans, and beat to combine.

7. Use the ice cream scoop to drop twenty-four equal-sized portions of dough onto the prepared cookie sheets, about 1 ½ inches apart.

8. Bake for 12 to 15 minutes, or until lightly golden around the edges and slightly soft in the center.

9. Remove from the oven and transfer to wire racks to cool completely.

f you were to put crumble topping on pretty much anything I think I could be convinced to eat it, even oysters . . . And I REALLY don't like oysters. Putting the crumble topping on pear ginger cake is a much better idea and I won't need any convincing whatsoever to eat it.

Pear Ginger Coffee Cake

CRUMBLE TOPPING

1 ½ cups all-purpose flour

½ cup dark brown sugar

½ cup granulated sugar

1 teaspoon ground ginger

½ teaspoon salt

¾ cup butter, chilled and cut into
    1-inch cubes

CAKE

1 ¾ cups pastry flour

1 teaspoon baking powder

1 teaspoon baking soda

½ teaspoon salt

½ cup butter, room temperature

1 ¼ cups granulated sugar

2 large eggs

1 cup sour cream, full fat

1 tablespoon freshly grated ginger

1 teaspoon pure vanilla

2 Bosc pears, peeled, cored and cut
    into ½-inch pieces

MAKES: 1 (9- x 13-inch) cake, about
    12 servings

YOU WILL NEED: 1 (9- x 13-inch)
    baking pan lined with parchment,
    pastry cutter

1. Preheat the oven to 350°F.

2. Prepare the crumble topping. In a small bowl, combine the all-purpose flour, both sugars, ground ginger and salt. Stir to combine. Use your pastry cutter or two knives to cut in the cold butter until large buttery crumbs form. Set aside.

3. For the cake, on a large piece of parchment paper, sift the pastry flour, baking powder, baking soda and salt. Set aside.

4. In a stand mixer fitted with a paddle attachment, cream the butter and sugar until light and fluffy. Scrape down the sides of the bowl.

5. Add the eggs one at a time, beating well after each addition. Scrape down the sides of the bowl. Add the sour cream, freshly grated ginger and vanilla. Beat again.

6. With the mixer running on low speed, add the dry ingredients and beat until well combined.

7. Add the chopped pears and beat again until just combined.

8. Pour the batter into the prepared pan and use a small offset spatula to spread it smoothly across the top. Sprinkle the crumb topping evenly over the batter.

9. Bake for 40 minutes, or until a wooden skewer inserted in the center of the cake comes out clean.

10. Remove the cake from the oven and allow it to cool in the pan for at least 20 minutes before slicing. It is wonderful served warm with whipped cream but just as great for breakfast with your morning coffee.

If you prefer a more classic combination, you could always replace the pear with approximately 1 cup of blueberries (fresh or frozen), use ground cinnamon instead of ground ginger in the crumble topping and use 1 teaspoon of cinnamon instead of 1 tablespoon of fresh ginger in the cake.

They say good fences make good neighbors, but I think good cake does a much better job.

Banana Pecan Caramel Cake

2 ½ cups pastry flour

1 ½ teaspoons ground cinnamon

1 ½ teaspoons baking soda

¾ teaspoon baking powder

½ teaspoon salt

3 large eggs

1 ½ cups vegetable oil

1 ½ cups granulated sugar

1 ½ teaspoons pure vanilla

1 ½ cups mashed bananas (about 3 bananas)

¾ cup chopped pecans

FINISHING TOUCHES

1 recipe Caramel Butter Cream (page 117)

MAKES: 1 (8-inch) four-layer cake, 8 to 12 servings

YOU WILL NEED: 2 (8-inch) circular cake pans, buttered and floured, rotating cake stand, large serrated knife

This cake is wonderful served on a plate with a big puddle of Caramel Sauce (page 126).

1. Preheat the oven to 350°F.

2. On a large piece of parchment paper, sift the flour, cinnamon, baking soda, baking powder and salt. Set aside.

3. In a stand mixer fitted with a paddle attachment, combine the eggs, oil, sugar and vanilla. Beat on high speed until well combined. Add the banana and mix again. Scrape down the sides of the bowl.

4. With the mixer running on low speed, add the dry ingredients and beat until just combined. Add the chopped pecans and beat again.

5. Divide the batter evenly between the prepared pans and use a small offset spatula to spread it smoothly across the top.

6. Bake for 40 to 45 minutes, or until a wooden skewer inserted in the center of a cake comes out clean.

7. Remove the cakes from the oven and allow them to cool in the pans for about 10 minutes before inverting them onto wire racks to cool completely. You may need to run a sharp knife around the edges of the pan if the cakes do not fall easily when first inverted.

8. While the cakes are cooling, prepare the Caramel Butter Cream.

9. Transfer the cakes to a rotating cake stand and use a large serrated knife to cut each cake in half on the horizontal to create four layers.

10. Place your bottom layer of the cake on a cake stand. Spread it generously with Caramel Butter Cream. Top with the next layer of cake and repeat. Continue in this fashion until all the layers are frosted. I like the effect of the bare edges of the cake layers with the butter cream peeking through.

Butter Creams and Frostings

*S*ome people call it frosting, some people call it icing, but my favorite name for it came from my nephew Max. He is a grown man now, but as a little boy he thought it was called "nice-ing," which makes perfect sense to me, because not much is nicer than a big pile of butter cream!

I strongly suggest making anything you can in advance to save you time and stress, but I find butter cream is best when made just prior to applying it. Fresh and fluffy butter cream is the easiest to work with, and if your butter is at room temperature, it takes only minutes to prepare. Butter cream that has been refrigerated takes on a dense and waxy appearance. It can be successfully revived by bringing it to room temperature and whipping it like crazy in the mixer before you use it, which means that in the end your advance prep really wouldn't have saved you much time at all.

 classic is a classic is a classic.

Vanilla Butter Cream

2 cups butter, room temperature

6 cups icing sugar

¼ cup whole milk

2 tablespoons pure vanilla

Seeds from 1 vanilla pod

MAKES: **About 5 cups, enough for 1 (8-inch) four-layer cake**

1. In a stand mixer fitted with a paddle attachment, beat the butter until very fluffy and pale yellow.

2. Turn the mixer speed to low and add the icing sugar. Continue to beat until well combined. Scrape down the sides of the bowl.

3. Add the milk, vanilla and vanilla seeds. Beat again. Turn the mixer speed to high and continue to beat until the icing is light and fluffy, approximately 10 minutes.

 truly delicious thing! For the best results, remember to always use full-fat cream cheese and not the spreadable or light kind.

Cream Cheese Butter Cream

1 cup butter, room temperature

½ cup cream cheese, full fat

3 cups icing sugar

1 tablespoon pure vanilla

MAKES: **About 4 cups, enough for 1 (8-inch) four-layer cake**

1. In a stand mixer fitted with a paddle attachment, cream the butter and cream cheese on high speed until light and fluffy.

2. Turn the mixer speed to low and add the icing sugar. Continue to beat until well combined. Scrape down the sides of the bowl and add the vanilla.

3. Turn the mixer speed to high and continue to beat until the icing is light and fluffy, 8 to 10 minutes.

Spreadable cream cheese contains a lot of air and water and the low-fat version contains even more. When you whip it the water will release, making your butter cream far too thin, not light and fluffy. Always, always use traditional full-fat cream cheese.

his combination of caramel and butter cream is like your two favorite people in the whole world getting married. You're happy for them, but even happier for yourself.

Caramel Butter Cream

½ cup Caramel Sauce (page 126)

1 cup butter, room temperature

4 cups icing sugar

2 tablespoons heavy cream

1 tablespoon pure vanilla

MAKES: **About 3 cups, enough for 1 (8-inch) four-layer cake**

1. Prepare the Caramel Sauce. Allow it to cool in the refrigerator for at least 2 hours. If the caramel is still warm it will melt the butter in your butter cream!

2. In a stand mixer fitted with a paddle attachment, cream the butter on high speed until very pale. Scrape down the sides of the bowl.

3. Turn the mixer speed to low and add the icing sugar. Scrape down the sides of the bowl.

4. Add the cream and vanilla and beat again. Add the caramel sauce and continue to beat on high speed until the butter cream is light and fluffy.

created this butter cream to top the Strawberry Cupcakes on page 84, but it would be equally delicious between the layers of a chocolate cake or on its own, by the spoonful. It counts as fruit, doesn't it?

Strawberry Butter Cream

1 cup butter, room temperature

4 cups icing sugar, sifted

½ cup seedless strawberry jam

1 tablespoon pure vanilla

1 tablespoon heavy cream

MAKES: **About 2 cups, enough for 1 dozen cupcakes**

1. In a stand mixer fitted with a paddle attachment, beat the butter on high speed until very pale. Stop the mixer and scrape down the sides of the bowl at least twice while beating the butter.

2. Turn the mixer speed to low and slowly add the icing sugar. Mix until well combined. Scrape down the sides of the bowl.

3. Add the strawberry jam, vanilla and cream. Beat to combine, then turn the mixer speed to high and continue beating until the butter cream is light and fluffy, 5 to 7 minutes.

*M*aybe it's the Italian in me, but I think this is one of the most delicious frostings out there. A traditional version has quite a bit more butter in it, but I find that can be a little overwhelming. Believe it or not, Butter's version has half the butter! Maybe this should be called Ironic Butter Cream.

Italian Butter Cream

1 ¼ cups granulated sugar

¼ cup water

6 egg whites

1 cup butter, room temperature, cut into 1-inch cubes

MAKES: **About 2 cups, enough for 1 (4- x 11-inch) four-layer cake or 1 dozen cupcakes**

YOU WILL NEED: **candy thermometer**

1. In a medium pot, place 1 cup of the sugar and the water. Give the sugar a stir with a spatula and then clip your candy thermometer to the side of the pot. Bring to a boil over high heat without stirring. Turn down the temperature slightly to maintain a low boil until the candy thermometer reads 240°F.

2. In a stand mixer fitted with a whisk attachment, beat the egg whites on medium speed until soft peaks form. (See page 18.) Slowly add the remaining ¼ cup sugar and then turn the mixer speed to high and whip until stiff peaks form.

3. Remove the pot of hot syrup from the heat. With the mixer running on low speed, slowly add the hot syrup to the egg whites. Try to avoid hitting the beaters with the syrup when adding it as it will spatter and could cause lumps.

4. Continue beating on medium speed until the egg whites are cool. You can then start to add the butter one piece at a time until it is all incorporated. The egg whites may appear to deflate once you start to add the butter, but don't panic. Continue beating until the butter starts to get fluffy and you will have a lovely silky Italian butter cream. You can now add your flavor options.

GINGERBREAD ITALIAN BUTTER CREAM

2 tablespoons fancy molasses

2 teaspoons pumpkin pie spice

COFFEE ITALIAN BUTTER CREAM

2 tablespoons espresso powder combined with 1 tablespoon hot water to create a coffee paste

CHOCOLATE ITALIAN BUTTER CREAM

1 teaspoon pure vanilla

½ cup dark chocolate chips, melted and cooled

*T*his butter cream takes on a slightly fuller flavor with the addition of the custard powder and is wonderful in combination with chocolate, but I also think it would be quite lovely paired with something fruity like Strawberry Cupcakes (page 84).

Custard Butter Cream

1 cup butter, room temperature

3 cups icing sugar

¼ cup custard powder

¼ cup whole milk

1 tablespoon pure vanilla

MAKES: **About 3 cups, enough for 1 dozen cupcakes**

1. In a stand mixer fitted with a paddle attachment, beat the butter on high speed until very pale. Scrape down the sides of the bowl at least twice while beating the butter.

2. Turn the mixer speed to low and slowly add the icing sugar and custard powder. Mix until well combined and then slowly add the milk and vanilla. Scrape down the sides of the bowl again.

3. Turn the mixer speed to high and beat until the icing is light and fluffy, about 10 minutes.

*M*ascarpone is a creamy Italian cheese with a subtle edge. Wonderful and rich, it makes a delicious addition to this butter cream.

Mascarpone Butter Cream

¾ cup butter, room temperature

1 cup mascarpone cheese

3 cups icing sugar

1 teaspoon pure vanilla

MAKES: **About 3 cups, enough for 1 dozen cupcakes**

1. In a stand mixer fitted with a paddle attachment, cream the butter on high speed for about 2 minutes. Add the mascarpone and beat again until well combined. Scrape down the sides of the bowl.

2. Turn the mixer speed to low and slowly add the icing sugar. Mix until well combined. Scrape down the sides of the bowl. Add the vanilla and beat again.

3. Turn the mixer speed to high and beat for another 5 minutes, or until the butter cream is light and fluffy.

*T*his recipe is a combination of two of my favorite things: champagne and butter cream. I should start combining more things I like. I'd like to start with shopping and money.

Champagne Butter Cream

1 cup butter, room temperature

3 cups icing sugar

6 tablespoons champagne

MAKES: **About 3 cups, enough for 1 dozen cupcakes**

1. In a stand mixer fitted with a paddle attachment, cream the butter and sugar on high speed until pale yellow. Scrape down the sides of the bowl.

2. Add the champagne and then continue beating until the butter cream is light and fluffy.

3. Make sure to pour yourself a little glass while you are working, because you don't want any of that champagne going to waste.

I had quite a bit of fun testing this recipe. At least I think I did. I don't really remember much from that day.

Bailey's Butter Cream

1 cup butter, room temperature

3 cups icing sugar

3 tablespoons Bailey's Irish Cream

MAKES: **About 3 cups, enough for 1 dozen cupcakes**

1. In a stand mixer fitted with a paddle attachment, cream the butter on high speed until very pale. Scrape down the sides of the bowl.

2. With the mixer running on low speed, slowly add the icing sugar. Beat to combine. Scrape down the sides of the bowl and add the Bailey's. Beat again.

3. Turn the mixer speed to high and beat for about 10 minutes, until the butter cream is light and fluffy.

*T*hank goodness beer doesn't taste as good as this butter cream. My friends might have to organize an intervention.

Guinness Butter Cream

3 cups icing sugar

½ cup dark cocoa

1 cup butter, room temperature

3 tablespoons Guinness

MAKES: **About 4 cups, enough for 1 (8-inch) four-layer cake**

1. On a large piece of parchment paper, sift the icing sugar and cocoa. Set aside.

2. In a stand mixer fitted with a paddle attachment, beat the butter on high speed until very pale. Scrape down the sides of the bowl.

3. Turn the mixer speed to low, and slowly add the icing sugar and cocoa. Mix until well combined and then add the beer. Scrape down the sides of the bowl again.

4. Turn the mixer speed to high and let it run for at least 10 minutes, until the butter cream is light and fluffy.

*W*hen you're working with royal icing, it is always a good idea to have a damp paper towel on hand to place over the bowl should you have to step away for a moment. If left exposed to the air, it will begin to set up and create little hard bits that don't look as nice on the finished product.

Royal Icing

2 cups icing sugar

2 tablespoons meringue powder

2 to 4 tablespoons water

MAKES: **Enough for 6 dozen (1-inch) cookies or 2 dozen (3-inch) cookies**

1. In a small bowl, sift together the icing sugar and meringue powder. Using a whisk or spoon, add the water 1 tablespoon at a time and stir until glossy and smooth.

A simple but delicious finishing touch to your éclairs or doughnuts, this glaze can be tinted any color and enhanced with other flavors to create lots of yummy options.

Vanilla Glaze

2 cups icing sugar

1 teaspoon pure vanilla

½ cup heavy cream

Food coloring of your choice

MAKES: **1 cup, enough for 1 dozen éclairs (see page 67) or to top 1 (9-inch) cake**

1. In a medium bowl, whisk together the icing sugar and vanilla with enough of the cream to make a glaze thin enough that it will spread nicely atop your éclair or doughnut once dipped but not so thin that it runs off the sides.

2. Add 1 to 2 drops of food coloring and whisk to create the color of your choice.

COFFEE GLAZE

Combine 1 tablespoon espresso powder with 1 teaspoon hot water to form a paste. Add to the sugar and cream in place of the vanilla.

CHOCOLATE GLAZE

In a small bowl, place 1 cup chocolate chips instead of the icing sugar. Warm the cream and vanilla in a small pot over medium heat until it just starts to bubble around the edges. Remove from the heat and pour over the chocolate chips. Allow the chocolate to sit for several minutes until the heat of the cream has caused it to melt. Stir until smooth.

MAPLE GLAZE

Replace ¼ cup of the heavy cream with ¼ cup pure maple syrup.

*T*his is a fun take on a traditional boiled icing that normally calls for white sugar and a little corn syrup. I have switched it up using some dark brown sugar and maple syrup, which gives it a wonderful depth of flavor and turns it the loveliest, softest shade of brown.

Brown Sugar Maple Frosting

1 ½ cups dark brown sugar

¼ cup water

¼ cup pure maple syrup

6 egg whites

½ cup granulated sugar

MAKES: 4 cups, enough for 1 (8-inch) four-layer cake

YOU WILL NEED: candy thermometer

See page 211 for tips on using up egg yolks.

1. In a small pot over medium heat, combine the brown sugar, water and maple syrup. Stir until the sugar has dissolved. Clip the candy thermometer to the side of the pot, turn the heat to high and bring the mixture to a boil.

2. Wash down the sides of the pan with a wet pastry brush to remove any sugar crystals that form. Measure the temperature with the candy thermometer and continue to boil until it reaches 230°F.

3. In a stand mixer fitted with a whisk attachment, beat the egg whites on high speed until soft peaks form. (See page 18.) Turn the mixer speed to medium and gradually add the granulated sugar 1 tablespoon at a time.

4. Turn the mixer speed to low and slowly add the hot sugar mixture, pouring it in a steady stream down the sides of the bowl. Let the mixer run until the frosting is cool and thick and shiny.

This icing is best used right away as it won't spread as nicely once it has cooled.

I created this to work with my Chocolate Whoopie Pies (page 23), but it would be insanely good on chocolate or vanilla cake.

Raspberry Fluff

2 tablespoons raspberry jam

1 ¾ cups granulated sugar

¼ cup water

1 tablespoon light corn syrup

4 egg whites

1 tablespoon Framboise (optional)

MAKES: **4 cups or enough for 1 dozen whoopie pies or 1 (8-inch) four-layer cake**

YOU WILL NEED: **candy thermometer**

This icing is best used right away as it won't spread as nicely once it has cooled.

1. Place the raspberry jam in a small bowl and microwave it briefly to warm, approximately 15 seconds, depending on the power of your microwave. You can also warm it over low heat in a pot. Place a strainer over a small bowl and strain the jam to remove any seeds. Set aside.

2. In a small pot over medium heat, combine 1 ½ cups of the sugar with the water and corn syrup. Stir until the sugar has dissolved. Clip your candy thermometer to the side of the pot. Turn up the heat and bring the syrup to a boil.

3. Wash down the sides of the pot with a wet pastry brush to remove any sugar crystals, which could cause lumps in your icing. Continue to boil until the candy thermometer reaches 230°F. Remove the pot from the heat.

4. In a stand mixer fitted with a whisk attachment, beat the egg whites on high speed until soft peaks form. (See page 18.) Turn the mixer speed to medium and slowly add the remaining ¼ cup sugar. Beat until stiff peaks have formed.

5. Turn the mixer speed to low and slowly add the hot syrup in a steady stream down the side of the bowl. Return the mixer speed to high and continue beating until the icing is thick and shiny.

6. Turn the mixer speed to low again and add the strained raspberry jam and Framboise, if you are using it. Beat again to combine.

The raspberry liqueur is optional, but it adds a lovely depth to the icing. You can also omit the raspberry jam and Framboise and replace it with 2 tablespoons pure vanilla for a simple vanilla fluff.

A lovely alternative to traditional butter cream on the exterior of a cake, this creates a shiny chocolate coating that screams elegance. Wait . . . Elegance would never scream. It merely nods politely when you look its way.

Chocolate Ganache

3 cups dark chocolate chips

2 tablespoons butter, room temperature

¼ cup whipping cream

MAKES: **3 cups, enough for 1 (4- x 11-inch) four-layer cake or 1 dozen cupcakes**

1. In a double boiler over medium heat, or a heatproof bowl placed over simmering water, melt the chocolate chips and butter.

2. Remove the chocolate from the heat and whisk in the cream. Allow the ganache to cool slightly before use.

3. The ganache can be made several days in advance and kept in the refrigerator. When you're ready to use it, place the bowl over a simmering pot of water to warm it through.

C aramel sauce is easy to make and keeps nicely in the refrigerator for a couple of weeks. If you are looking for a quick way to improve a bowl of vanilla ice cream here would be your answer.

Caramel Sauce

1 ¼ cup granulated sugar

¼ cup water

1 cup heavy cream

1 tablespoon butter

MAKES: **About 2 cups**

YOU WILL NEED: **A medium-sized heavy bottomed saucepan, small pastry brush**

1. Place the sugar and water in a medium-sized heavy bottomed saucepan. Place over medium-high heat. Dip your pastry brush in water and use it to wash away any sugar crystals that may form on the sides of the pan.

2. Bring the sugar to a boil without stirring. Continue to boil until the sugar starts to caramelize and turns a lovely golden brown.

3. Remove from the heat. Add the cream and whisk to combine. Be careful as you do this as it may spit a little when you add the cream.

4. Add the butter and whisk again.

This caramel sauce will keep sealed in the refrigerator for up to 3 weeks. You can rewarm it over low heat or in the microwave for serving.

Summer Celebrations

The last day of school, the country, dads, long days and warm nights, shorts and flip flops, the sound of the ice cream truck, freshly cut grass, a run through the sprinkler, bare feet, hot dogs at a ball game, corn on the cob, back-lane berry picking, front porches, picnics, sand castles, the hum of the fan and road trips with the windows down . . .

Let's celebrate it all. Fall is only a few pages away.

*A*lways a tough one to explain. This cake is mostly vanilla with a little chocolate and then just to add to the confusion, we color it red. As strange as it all sounds, once you take your first bite it will make perfect sense.

Red Velvet Cake

2 cups whole walnuts

¼ cup dark cocoa

¼ cup boiling water

2 tablespoons red food coloring

2 ¼ cups pastry flour

1 teaspoon salt

½ cup butter, room temperature

1 ½ cups granulated sugar

2 large eggs

1 teaspoon pure vanilla

1 cup buttermilk

1 teaspoon baking soda

1 tablespoon white vinegar

FINISHING TOUCHES
Cream Cheese Butter Cream
    (page 116)

MAKES: 1 (8-inch) two-layer cake,
    8 to 12 slices

YOU WILL NEED: 2 (8-inch) circular
    cake pans, buttered and floured
    1 (11- x 17-inch) rimmed cookie
    sheet lined with parchment paper

1. Preheat the oven to 350°F.

2. Spread the walnuts across the prepared tray and bake for 10 minutes, or until nicely golden. You can use a metal spatula to give them a turn at the halfway mark so they toast evenly. Remove them from the oven and allow them to cool before roughly chopping.

3. In a small bowl, combine the cocoa, boiling water and red food coloring. Whisk to combine, being careful, as you don't want it splashing all over your counter! Set aside.

4. On a large piece of parchment paper, sift together the flour and salt. Set aside.

5. In a stand mixer fitted with a paddle attachment, cream the butter on medium speed until light and fluffy. Scrape down the sides of the bowl. Add the sugar, eggs and vanilla and beat again until well combined. Scrape down the sides of the bowl.

6. Turn the mixer speed to low and add the cocoa mixture. Continue to beat until combined. Scrape down the sides of the bowl.

7. Add the flour and buttermilk alternately, beginning and ending with the flour. Scrape down the sides of the bowl. Add the baking soda and then the vinegar and beat again.

8. Divide the batter evenly between the two prepared pans.

9. Bake for 25 to 30 minutes, or until a wooden skewer inserted in the center of a cake comes out clean.

10. Remove the cakes from the oven, allow them to cool in the pans for about 10 minutes and then invert them onto wire racks

to cool completely. You may need to run a sharp knife around the edges of the pans if the cakes do not easily fall when first inverted.

11. Meanwhile, prepare the Cream Cheese Butter Cream.

12. Transfer your first cake layer to a cake stand. Use an offset spatula to spread the butter cream generously across the layer. Top with your second layer and continue to cover the top and sides with a nice smooth layer of butter cream. Don't worry too much about perfection as the toasted walnuts will hide a lot of flaws!

13. Once the cake is covered in butter cream, scoop up large handfuls of the chopped toasted nuts and press them into the sides of the cake. It helps to place your cake stand on a cookie sheet to catch any falling walnuts, which you can then scoop up and use again.

This is the perfect summer treat to pack for a picnic in the park. It's like a portable rhubarb crisp, so if you can find a way to bring along a few scoops of vanilla ice cream, I'd suggest that too.

Rhubar

4 cups rhubarb, fresh or frozen, cut in ½-inch pieces

1 cup granulated sugar

1 tablespoon cornstarch

1 teaspoon pure vanilla

1 cup butter, room temperature

1 cup dark brown sugar

2 cups all-purpose flour

1 cup large-flake rolled oats

1 teaspoon baking powder

½ teaspoon baking soda

½ teaspoon salt

MAKES: **16 bars**

YOU WILL NEED: **1 (9- x 9-inch) baking pan, buttered and lined with parchment paper**

STORAGE: **The bars will keep in an airtight container for up to 1 week or in the freezer for up to 3 months.**

1. Preheat the oven to 350°F.

2. In a medium pot over medium-high heat, combine the rhubarb and sugar. Cook, stirring occasionally, until the rhubarb has broken down to a chunky jam. This should take 10 to 20 minutes (frozen will take a little more time to break down). Turn down the heat to low. Place a couple of tablespoons of the hot rhubarb mixture in a small bowl with the cornstarch and stir to combine, making sure there are no lumps of cornstarch. Add the cornstarch mixture back in with the rest of the rhubarb, stirring to combine. Boil gently until thickened. Remove from the heat and set aside.

3. When the rhubarb has cooled slightly, add the vanilla and stir to combine. Set aside.

4. In a stand mixer fitted with a paddle attachment, cream the butter and sugar until light and fluffy. Scrape down the sides of the bowl.

5. Add the flour, oats, baking powder, baking soda and salt and continue mixing on medium speed until well combined.

6. Divide the dough into two and press half into the prepared pan firmly and evenly. Spread the rhubarb mixture evenly across the bottom layer.

7. Crumble the remaining half of the dough across the top of the rhubarb.

8. Bake for 30 to 35 minutes, or until the top layer is a lovely golden brown.

9. Remove the pan from the oven and allow the rhubar to cool completely in the pan before cutting it into sixteen bars.

I remember as a child how much I enjoyed the summer holidays. I knew I had reached an important milestone the day I was allowed to run, all on my own and barefoot, to the corner store with a fist full of coins. Once there, I would have the challenging task of deciding what to treat myself to. The original version of this cupcake often won out, and as a kid I didn't mind that I couldn't pronounce all the strange ingredients it was filled with. As an adult, I do mind. So I created this version and now I don't have to run all the way to the store in my bare feet.

Cupcakes with the Most-ess
(inspired by our friends at Hostess)

CUPCAKES

1 ½ cups all-purpose flour

⅓ cup dark cocoa

½ teaspoon baking powder

½ teaspoon baking soda

½ teaspoon salt

½ cup butter, room temperature

¾ cup granulated sugar

2 large eggs

1 cup buttermilk

1 teaspoon pure vanilla

FILLING

½ cup whole milk

1 tablespoon all-purpose flour

1 cup butter, room temperature

2 cups icing sugar

1 teaspoon pure vanilla

FINISHING TOUCHES

1 recipe Chocolate Ganache
(page 126)

MAKES: **1 dozen cupcakes**

1. Preheat the oven to 350°F.

2. For the cupcakes, on a large piece of parchment paper, sift the flour, cocoa, baking powder, baking soda and salt. Set aside.

3. In a stand mixer fitted with a paddle attachment, cream the butter and sugar on medium-high speed until light and fluffy. Scrape down the sides of the bowl.

4. Add the eggs one at a time, beating well after each addition. Scrape down the sides of the bowl.

5. Add the buttermilk and vanilla and beat to combine.

6. With the mixer running on low speed, slowly add the dry ingredients and beat until combined.

7. Use the ice cream scoop to fill each muffin cup three-quarters full.

8. Bake for 15 to 20 minutes, or until a wooden skewer inserted in the center of a cupcake comes out clean.

9. Remove the cupcakes from the oven and allow them to cool in the pan for about 10 minutes before gently placing them on wire racks to cool completely.

10. Meanwhile, prepare the filling. In a small pot over medium heat, combine the milk and flour and whisk until the mixture starts to thicken, about 5 minutes. Set aside to cool.

YOU WILL NEED: 1 muffin pan, buttered and floured, large ice cream scoop, 14-inch piping bag fitted with a small plain tip, 1 (11- x 17-inch) rimmed cookie sheet lined with parchment paper

These cupcakes would also be delicious filled with the Raspberry Fluff icing (page 125).

11. In a stand mixer fitted with a paddle attachment, cream the butter and icing sugar until pale yellow. Scrape down the sides of the bowl.

12. Add the cooled milk and vanilla and beat on high speed until light and fluffy. Fill the prepared piping bag with this mixture.

13. Prepare the Chocolate Ganache and pour it into a bowl that is deep enough for you to submerge a cupcake in it.

14. Push the tip of your piping bag through the bottom of a cupcake and squeeze gently until the cupcake starts to swell. Don't squeeze too hard or the cupcake may split from too much filling. Repeat with all the cupcakes. Reserve the balance of the filling in the bag for decorating the top of the cupcakes.

15. Once all the cupcakes have been filled, drop them one by one in the ganache. Use a fork to gently lift the cupcake from the ganache and tap it on the edge of the bowl to help remove any excess (not that I believe there could ever be an excess of ganache!). Transfer each dipped cupcake to the prepared tray and use a knife to help slide the cupcake off the fork.

16. Place the cupcakes in the refrigerator for about 20 minutes to help the ganache set. Once it has set, you can pipe the top of each cupcake with a little more filling for decoration.

*N*anaimo Bars are truly Canadian and truly delicious. You can find the recipe for them in my first book, *Butter Baked Goods* (read: shameless plug for my first book), but should you, for reasons I can't imagine, not have that book on hand, I have created a version in cupcake form with all the same yummy elements.

Nanaimo Bar Cupcakes

1 ¼ cups all-purpose flour

½ cup dark cocoa

1 teaspoon baking soda

½ teaspoon salt

½ cup butter, room temperature

½ cup granulated sugar

½ cup dark brown sugar

1 large egg

¾ cup whole milk

⅓ cup sour cream, full fat

3 tablespoons brewed coffee

1 teaspoon pure vanilla

½ cup unsweetened shredded coconut chips

½ cup walnuts, chopped

FINISHING TOUCHES

1 cup dark chocolate

1 recipe Custard Butter Cream (page 120)

MAKES: 1 dozen cupcakes

YOU WILL NEED: 1 muffin pan lined with paper liners, large ice cream scoop, 14-inch piping bag fitted with a large plain tip, 1 ½-inch circular cutter, 1 (11- x 17-inch) rimmed cookie sheet lined with parchment paper

1. Preheat the oven to 350°F.

2. On a large piece of parchment paper, sift the flour, cocoa, baking soda and salt. Set aside.

3. In a stand mixer fitted with a paddle attachment, cream the butter and both sugars on medium-high speed until light and fluffy. Scrape down the sides of the bowl.

4. Add the egg and beat well. Scrape down the sides of the bowl.

5. In a large liquid measuring cup, combine the milk, sour cream, coffee and vanilla. Whisk to combine.

6. With the mixer running on low speed, add the dry ingredients in three additions, alternating with the liquid in two additions. Scrape down the sides of the bowl.

7. Remove the bowl from the stand and gently fold in the coconut and walnuts.

8. Use the ice cream scoop to fill each paper liner about three-quarters full with batter.

9. Bake for 20 to 25 minutes, or until a wooden skewer inserted in the center of a cupcake comes out clean.

10. Meanwhile, prepare the chocolate toppers. In a double boiler over medium heat, or a small heatproof bowl set over simmering water, melt the chocolate chips. Pour the melted chocolate onto the prepared cookie sheet and use a small offset spatula to spread it in a circle in the center of the tray, about ⅛ inch thick.

11. Place the tray in the refrigerator to set up, approximately 15 minutes.

12. Once the chocolate has set, use your circular cutter to cut 12 disks in the chocolate, but don't try to lift them out at this point. Place the tray back in the refrigerator.

13. Remove the cupcakes from the oven and allow them to cool in the pan for 10 minutes, then transfer them to wire racks to cool completely.

14. Meanwhile, prepare the Custard Butter Cream.

15. Fill the piping bag with the butter cream and pipe some over the top of each cupcake. You can also use your small offset spatula to spread the icing if you don't have a piping bag handy.

16. Remove the tray of chocolate from the refrigerator and gently lift off the chocolate disks. This should be very easy to do when they are chilled. Top each cupcake with a chocolate disk and press very lightly to make it adhere.

think No-Stress Pie would be a better name for this dessert given how simple it is to make, with the most impressive results. Strawberry and basil make a winning combination but this recipe does allow for you to switch up the fruit and create your own combinations. Peach rosemary anyone?

Strawberry Basil Galette

1 recipe Everyday Pastry (page 141)

1 lb. strawberries, stems removed, washed, dried and halved (approximately 3 cups once cut)

1 cup granulated sugar

¼ cup fresh basil leaves, finely chopped

1 tablespoon tapioca

1 tablespoon cornstarch

¼ teaspoon salt

2 tablespoons butter, chilled and cut into 4 pieces

FINISHING TOUCHES

1 large egg, beaten

1 tablespoon water

Coarse sanding sugar

MAKES: 1 galette, 8 to 10 slices

YOU WILL NEED: 1 (11- x 17-inch) rimmed cookie sheet lined with parchment paper

1. Prepare the Everyday Pastry.

2. Preheat the oven to 350°F.

3. In a large bowl, combine the strawberries, sugar, basil, tapioca, cornstarch and salt. Gently stir to evenly coat the fruit.

4. On a lightly floured work surface, use a rolling pin to roll out a chilled disk of pastry. Roll from the center of the dough out toward the edges, rotating the dough every few strokes to make sure it doesn't stick. Lightly dust the work surface with more flour as needed. Continue to roll until you have a circle of dough about 16 inches in diameter and ⅛ inch thick.

5. At this point you will need to fold the dough into quarters and transfer it to the prepared cookie sheet as you won't be able to transfer it once you have filled it with fruit. Carefully unfold the pastry on the tray.

6. Spoon the strawberries, or fruit of your choice (see page 140), onto the center of the pastry in a mound about 10 inches in diameter. Dot the fruit with the chilled butter pieces.

7. Begin to fold the remaining dough onto the top of the galette, making a tuck every 2 inches or so. There is no stress here because you really can't mess this up. The very nature of the galette is that it should look rustic and free-form. We aren't looking for precision here. Once all the dough has been folded over, you should have a little circular window left on top, exposing the lovely fruit.

8. Make an egg wash. In a small bowl, combine the egg and water and beat with a fork to combine. Use a pastry brush to coat the top and sides of the pastry with the egg wash. Sprinkle liberally with the sanding sugar.

9. Bake for about 1 hour, or until the fruit is bubbling up in the middle.

10. Remove the galette from the oven and allow to cool completely on the pan before transferring it to a cake stand or large platter. Should you be a little nervous about the transfer, remember that you could slide the whole galette on the very parchment paper it was baked on from the baking sheet to a platter and serve it from there, only adding to the rustic effect we were aiming for.

Flavor Options

PEACH ROSEMARY

3 cups peaches, peeled and cut into 1-inch cubes
1 tablespoon fresh rosemary leaves, finely chopped

BLUEBERRY LEMON

3 cups fresh blueberries
1 tablespoon lemon zest

RASPBERRY MINT

3 cups fresh raspberries
5 mint leaves, finely chopped

The perfect pastry to have on hand for everyday life. You can use it for sweet and savory baking alike, whether you are making a strawberry galette or have a hankering for a chicken pie.

If you are making chicken pie, please call me. I love chicken pie.

Everyday Pastry

2 ½ cups all-purpose flour

½ teaspoon salt

Zest of 1 lemon (you can omit this for savory baking but personally I think it would give the chicken pie a little zip . . . just saying)

1 cup butter, chilled and cut into 1-inch cubes

1 large egg

¼ cup cold water (you may find you need a tablespoon or so more depending on the day or weather or your mood—absolutely fine.)

1 tablespoon lemon juice

MAKES: enough for 1 double-crust pie or 2 (10-inch) galettes

YOU WILL NEED: pastry cutter

STORAGE: You can store the dough wrapped tightly in the refrigerator for up to 3 days or in the freezer for up to 1 month.

1. In a large bowl, combine the flour, salt and lemon zest. Scatter the butter bits over the top of the flour mixture. Use your pastry cutter to cut in the cold butter until the mixture forms large pea-sized crumbs. You should still be able to recognize some of the butter.

2. In a small bowl, combine the egg, water and lemon juice. Whisk to combine, then pour over the flour mixture.

3. Mix with a fork until the dough starts to come together. Gently use your hands to finish mixing the dough until it comes together enough to shape.

4. Shape the dough into two evenly sized disks about ½ inch thick and wrap each one separately in plastic wrap. Refrigerate for at least 2 hours, or overnight, before using.

*D*eanut butter lovers and squirrels, lend me your ear! I have created a pie just for you! A perfect treat to make during the warm summer months as I'd rather hang around the refrigerator than around a hot oven.

Squirrel Pie

½ cup plus 2 tablespoons butter

1 ½ cups chocolate crumbs

1 ¼ cups icing sugar

1 ½ cups heavy cream

1 teaspoon pure vanilla

Two 8-ounce packages cream cheese, full fat

1 cup smooth peanut butter

¾ cup dark chocolate chips

2 tablespoons roasted and salted peanuts, chopped

MAKES: 1 (7-inch) pie, 8 to 12 slices

YOU WILL NEED: 1 (7-inch) spring-form pan, buttered

STORAGE: This pie is best stored in the refrigerator to keep it nice and firm, which makes cutting and serving much easier.

1. Preheat the oven to 350°F.

2. In a small pot over medium heat or in your microwave, melt ½ cup of the butter. Remove it from the heat and allow to cool slightly.

3. In a medium bowl, combine the chocolate crumbs and melted butter and stir to combine.

4. Place the chocolate crumbs in the prepared pan and use your hands to press and evenly coat the bottom and sides to create the shell. Once all the sides have been coated, use a flat-bottomed, straight-sided glass or jar to help smooth out the shell and compress it by running it over the bottom and up against the sides of the pan while pressing lightly.

5. Bake for 10 minutes. Remove the shell from the oven and set it aside to cool. Turn off the oven, because that's the last we'll be needing it!

6. Once the shell has cooled completely, you can release it from the pan and transfer it to a serving plate.

7. In a stand mixer fitted with a whisk attachment, whip the cream, ¼ cup icing sugar and vanilla until quite stiff. It should hold up nicely on a spoon. Scrape the whipped cream into a large bowl and set aside.

8. Return the bowl to the stand mixer and swap out your whisk for a paddle attachment. Cream the cream cheese and peanut butter on high speed until well combined. Scrape down the sides of the bowl. Turn the mixer speed to low and add the remaining cup of icing sugar, mixing until combined. Turn the mixer speed to high and continue to beat until light and fluffy.

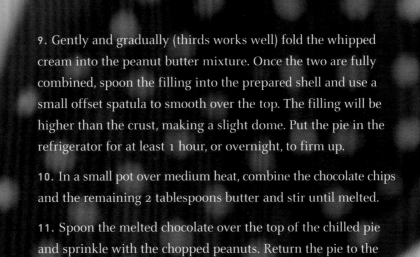

9. Gently and gradually (thirds works well) fold the whipped cream into the peanut butter mixture. Once the two are fully combined, spoon the filling into the prepared shell and use a small offset spatula to smooth over the top. The filling will be higher than the crust, making a slight dome. Put the pie in the refrigerator for at least 1 hour, or overnight, to firm up.

10. In a small pot over medium heat, combine the chocolate chips and the remaining 2 tablespoons butter and stir until melted.

11. Spoon the melted chocolate over the top of the chilled pie and sprinkle with the chopped peanuts. Return the pie to the refrigerator until the chocolate has set, about 15 minutes. Holler for your squirrel friends and start serving!

Zelda's Birthday Party

The story of Zelda is a funny one. In November 2012, Paul, India and I were in Los Angeles for the weekend, just a little getaway. We were roaming the farmers' market, taking in the sights. A dog rescue society had set up shop in the market with lots of little dogs looking for homes. India and I spied Miss Z and something clicked. Paul didn't have the same reaction, and when we suggested that we bring her home with us, he responded with a firm and decisive "NO." But slowly and surely, I convinced Paul to see the light. Or maybe I just wore him down. Regardless, two weeks later we picked Zelda up at the airport, a nervous little thing that didn't know what to make of all these Canadians. She came to us with little information about her past, but that's the magic of a rescue dog. There is a lot of guessing and a little bit of imagination when trying to piece together their history, but not much of that really matters. What matters is that Zelda found a home and a huge place in our hearts. Oh, and Paul Daykin? He's Zelda's biggest fan.

I just love being right.

ruth be told, little Miss Z would pretty much eat anything you put in front of her. I like to say she has an adventurous spirit and a keen willingness to try new food items, but really, based on how fast it disappears, I'm pretty sure she has no idea what she is inhaling most of the time. With that in mind, I made sure to load her birthday cake up with lots of peanut butter and bacon in the hopes that she would stop and savor it a little. Nope. It was gone in a flash, but the peanut butter kept her licking her lips for quite a while.

Zeldacakes

2 strips bacon

1 cup whole wheat flour

1 teaspoon baking soda

1 cup apple sauce

¾ cup peanut butter

¾ cup grated carrot

¼ cup vegetable oil

¼ cup cream cheese

MAKES: ½ dozen Zeldacakes

YOU WILL NEED: 1 muffin pan lined with 6 paper liners, large ice cream scoop, 10-inch piping bag fitted with a large star tip, 1 (11- x 17-inch) rimmed cookie sheet lined with parchment paper

1. Preheat the oven to 350°F.

2. Place the bacon on the prepared cookie sheet and bake for approximately 10 minutes. Turn the strips over and continue to bake until the bacon is cooked through and slightly crispy. Remove the tray from the oven and transfer the bacon strips to a piece of paper towel. (Leave the oven on.)

3. Once cool, finely chop one strip of bacon and break the other strip into six random bits. Set aside.

4. In a large bowl, place the flour, baking soda, apple sauce, ¼ cup of the peanut butter, chopped bacon, carrot and oil. Use a wooden spoon or spatula to stir until well combined.

5. Use the ice cream scoop to divide the batter evenly between the six muffin cups.

6. Bake for 20 minutes, or until a wooden skewer inserted in the center of a Zeldacake comes out clean.

7. Remove the cakes from the oven and allow them to cool slightly in the pan before transferring them to a wire rack to cool completely.

8. In a stand mixer fitted with a paddle attachment, cream the remaining ½ cup peanut butter and the cream cheese until well combined. Fill your prepared piping bag with the doggy icing.

9. Pipe the top of each cake with a little mound of icing and top with a piece of the remaining bacon.

*P*aul describes Zelda as a mixed breed: part torpedo and part bratwurst. She gets her torpedo side from her ability to dive bomb, at great speed, into bed with us every morning and well, her sausage-like looks might just come from eating one too many of these cookies.

Zelda's Favorite Cookies

4 strips bacon

2 cups whole wheat flour

⅓ cup peanut butter

2 tablespoons honey

2 tablespoons parsley, finely chopped

1 large egg

½ cup water

MAKES: **5 dozen cookies**

YOU WILL NEED: **1 (11- x 17-inch) rimmed cookie sheet lined with parchment paper, 2-inch cookie cutters (Zelda likes her cookies shaped liked cats and bones)**

STORAGE: **These will easily keep in an airtight container for up to 1 month.**

1. Preheat the oven to 350°F.

2. Using a large chef's knife, finely dice the bacon. Place it in a medium skillet over medium-high heat and cook until the bacon bits are quite crispy.

3. In a stand mixer fitted with a paddle attachment, combine the bacon, any residual fat from the skillet and the remaining ingredients. Turn the mixer speed to medium-high and beat until well combined.

4. On a lightly floured work surface, use a rolling pin to roll the dough to about ¼ inch thick.

5. Use the cookie cutter of your dog's choice to cut out as many cookies as you can, then reroll the scraps and repeat until you have used up all the dough.

6. Place the cookies on the prepared cookie sheets and bake for 18 to 20 minutes, or until the cookies are quite dry and crunchy.

7. Remove from the oven and transfer the cookies to wire racks to cool before sharing with your hound. You don't want any burnt tongues.

I have always said that if I could have one superpower, it would be the power to speak to animals, just like Dr. Doolittle. I'd love to learn about Zelda's past and what our cats get up to on their adventures throughout the day. Of course, what if they told me they didn't liked being kissed so much or didn't like me speaking to them in that high, squeaky voice I use? Oh dear.

Peanut Butter Dog Bones

1 cup peanut butter

½ cup mashed banana

½ cup almond milk

2 cups whole wheat flour

1 cup large-flake oats

1 teaspoon baking powder

MAKES: **15 (4-inch) dog bone cookies**

YOU WILL NEED: **1 (11- x 17-inch) rimmed cookie sheet lined with parchment paper, 4-inch dog bone cookie cutter**

STORAGE: **These will keep in an airtight container for up to 2 weeks.**

1. Preheat the oven to 350°F.

2. In a stand mixer fitted with a paddle attachment, combine the peanut butter, banana and almond milk and beat to combine. Scrape down the sides of the bowl.

3. With the mixer running on low speed, add the flour, oats and baking powder. Beat to combine. Turn the mixer speed to high and beat for a few minutes more to ensure the dough has pulled together.

4. Turn the dough out onto a lightly floured work surface and knead it for several minutes to ensure it has come together. Use your rolling pin to roll the dough about ¼ inch thick.

5. Cut out the cookies with your cookie cutter. Reroll the scraps and cut again until you have used up all your dough. Don't worry about the dough getting too tough as you reroll it—your doggie won't mind a crunchy cookie.

6. Place the cookies on the prepared cookie sheet and bake for 30 minutes, or until lightly browned and quite crisp.

7. Remove the cookies from the oven and allow them to cool before sharing with your four-legged friend.

*T*he perfect little treat for all Zelda's friends. I mean, it wouldn't be a party without loot bags!

Sweet Potato Chews

2 large sweet potatoes

Olive oil

Salt and pepper

MAKES: **About 3 dozen chews**

YOU WILL NEED: **2 (11- x 17-inch) rimmed cookie sheets lined with parchment paper**

1. Preheat the oven to 325°F.

2. Wash and dry the sweet potatoes. Using a large knife or mandolin, cut the sweet potatoes into rounds about $1/8$ inch thick.

3. Spread the sweet potato rounds in one layer across the prepared trays. Drizzle with a little olive oil and sprinkle with salt and pepper.

4. Bake for about 1 hour, or until the chews are crisp and a toasty brown. It is a good idea to flip the chews at least once during the hour to ensure even baking.

5. Remove from the oven and allow the chews to cool on the trays before sharing. I suggest sharing because these chips make a tasty little snack for humans as well dogs. You may want to indulge on the sly, though, because I noticed Zelda gave me the stink eye when she caught me snacking on them.

These treats will keep in an airtight container for up to 2 weeks, but if your dog is anything like Zelda and her friends, they will be gone long before that.

Halloween

Some people are just born to wear a costume. They love every moment of it, from the planning to the creation to the big reveal. And some, of course, are not. I'm not sure at what point this trait develops in a human. It must be before birth, because I'm pretty sure that first moment when our daughter, India, entered this world and came out screaming, what she was really upset about was the prospect of one day being forced to wear a costume. It was never her thing. I mean, what three-year-old doesn't want to dress up as a bumblebee? Miss India, that's who. She was one annoyed little bee. Somewhere around Grade 1 she agreed to a very simple witch costume and continued to wear it for many years to come. We didn't need to mark the door jamb with her height but rather her legs as the hemline rose. But regardless of where you stand on costumes, to wear or not to wear, the common ground we can all find isn't one populated with zombies and naughty nurses. It's an island made of tiny chocolate bars, caramel apples and peanut butter cups. For little else matters when you find yourself holding a pillowcase full of candy.

*T*made my first doughnut at the ripe old age of forty-five. It's a good thing I waited this long to start, because based on how many I have consumed in the last three days it freaks me out a little to think what that number might be if I'd started at forty-four. If your willpower is stronger than mine, these doughnuts will keep, when tightly wrapped, for up to 3 days.

Pumpkin Cinnamon Sugar Doughnuts

CINNAMON SUGAR

2 cups granulated sugar

2 tablespoons ground cinnamon

DOUGHNUTS

1 ½ cups all-purpose flour, plus extra for kneading

1 ½ teaspoons baking powder

½ teaspoon ground cinnamon

½ teaspoon salt

¼ teaspoon ground allspice

½ cup granulated sugar

2 tablespoons butter, room temperature

½ cup canned pumpkin

1 large egg

MAKES: 1 dozen doughnuts (and 1 dozen doughnut holes!)

YOU WILL NEED: an electric deep-fryer, 1 (11- x 17-inch) rimmed cookie sheet lined with parchment paper, 1 (11- x 17-inch) rimmed cookie sheet lined with paper towel, 2- to 3-inch circular doughnut cutter (or you can use a 2- to 3-inch circular cutter and a 1-inch circular cutter to make the holes)

1. Follow the instructions for preparing your deep-fryer. I like to use a vegetable shortening to fry the doughnuts. Set the temperature gauge to 350°F.

2. For the cinnamon sugar, in a large bowl, combine the sugar and cinnamon and set aside.

3. For the doughnuts, on a large piece of parchment paper, sift the flour, baking powder, cinnamon, salt and allspice. Set aside.

4. In a stand mixer fitted with a paddle attachment, combine the sugar and butter and beat on medium speed. Scrape down the sides of the bowl and add the pumpkin and egg. Beat again until well combined.

5. Turn the mixer speed to low and slowly add the dry ingredients. Continue beating until just combined.

6. Turn the dough out onto a lightly floured work surface. It will be a little sticky as it is a soft dough. Give it a few kneads and add a little flour as you go. Use a rolling pin to gently roll the dough out to about ½ inch thick. Dip your cutter in flour and use it to cut out as many doughnuts and doughnut holes as you can and then reroll the scraps and repeat until all the dough has been used. Place the doughnuts on the tray lined with parchment.

7. Once the oil has reached the desired temperature, very gently place a couple of doughnuts in the oil, being careful to not drop them in. You don't want to get splashed with hot oil. Allow the doughnuts to cook for 1 to 2 minutes per side (the doughnut holes will cook quicker because they are so much smaller). Use a metal slotted spoon to help turn the doughnuts over at the halfway point. Once they're cooked, carefully lift the doughnuts

and transfer them to the bowl of cinnamon sugar. Use another spoon to sprinkle the sugar over the top and sides of the doughnut and then gently lift it from the sugar and place it atop the tray lined with paper towel. Repeat with the balance of the doughnuts.

You can always deep-fry without the use of an electric deep-fryer by filling a large, deep, heavy-bottomed pot with vegetable oil or shortening and using your candy thermometer to establish the correct temperature when heating the oil, but this method does prove really challenging when trying to keep the oil temperature consistent. I much prefer the cleanliness, safety and convenience of the self-contained appliance.

These are such a fun treat to make for Halloween parties. Stacked up on a cake stand, they make for a very creepy but delicious centerpiece.

Witchey Fingers

½ cup butter, room temperature

¾ cup icing sugar

1 large egg

½ teaspoon pure vanilla

½ teaspoon almond extract

2 cups all-purpose flour

½ teaspoon baking powder

½ teaspoon salt

2 drops green food coloring

18 blanched whole almonds

¼ cup raspberry jam

MAKES: 1 ½ dozen cookies

YOU WILL NEED: 2 (11- x 17-inch) rimmed cookie sheets lined with parchment paper

STORAGE: These cookies will keep in an airtight container for up to 1 week or in the freezer for up to 3 months. (Though I find it strange that you might have a hankering for a witchey finger in January.)

1. Preheat the oven to 350°F.

2. In a stand mixer fitted with a paddle attachment, cream the butter and sugar on medium speed until light and fluffy. Scrape down the sides of the bowl. Add the egg and beat to combine.

3. Scrape down the sides of the bowl, add the vanilla and almond extract and beat again.

4. With the mixer running on low speed, slowly add the flour, baking powder and salt and beat until combined. Add the green food coloring and continue beating until it is evenly distributed and your dough is the color of a witch's finger.

5. Remove the dough from the mixer and shape it into a rectangle. Cut the dough into eighteen even pieces and roll each piece into a little log approximately 1 inch wide and 4 inches long.

6. Place each cookie onto the prepared cookie sheets about ½ inch apart. Press a blanched almond into the end of each cookie to form the nail. Use two fingers to press down lightly into the middle of the cookie to create the knuckle.

7. Bake the cookies for 10 to 12 minutes, or until they are just turning a light brown and are firm to the touch.

8. Remove the cookies from the oven and allow them to cool slightly on the trays before transferring them to wire racks to cool completely. While the cookies are still slightly warm, lift off the almonds and set them aside.

9. Place a small amount of raspberry jam, approximately ½ teaspoon, into the indentation the almond left on each cookie. Place the almond on top of the jam and press lightly. The jam will peek out from under the almond, giving the spooky effect we are aiming for.

*I*f you were to create a holiday recognition game using only candy as the clue, the second you held up a tiny piece of candy corn everyone would race to smack their buzzer and scream, "Halloween for 100 points!!" Okay, clearly that clue was too easy, but it still sounds like a pretty fun game.

White Chocolate Candy Corn Sandwich Cookies

½ cup butter, room temperature

1 ½ cups icing sugar

2 large eggs

½ teaspoon pure vanilla

3 cups pastry flour

1 to 2 drops yellow food coloring

1 to 2 drops red food coloring

½ cup white chocolate chips

1 cup candy corn

MAKES: 2 dozen sandwich cookies

YOU WILL NEED: 2 (11- x 17-inch) rimmed cookie sheets lined with parchment paper, 2-inch circular cookie cutter

STORAGE: These cookies will keep in an airtight container for up to 1 week.

1. In a stand mixer fitted with a paddle attachment, cream the butter and icing sugar on high speed until light and fluffy. Scrape down the sides of the bowl.

2. Turn the mixer speed to medium and add the eggs one at a time, beating well after each addition. Scrape down the sides of the bowl. Add the vanilla and beat again.

3. With the mixer running on low speed, slowly add the flour and beat until combined.

4. Add the yellow food coloring to the dough and beat until fully incorporated.

5. Scoop out half of the dough and place it in a small bowl. Set aside.

6. Turn the mixer back on at low speed and add the red food coloring to the balance of the dough to turn it orange. Continue beating until fully incorporated.

7. Shape each piece of dough into a disk and wrap them separately in plastic wrap. Chill the dough for at least 1 hour in the refrigerator.

8. Preheat the oven to 350°F.

9. Place one of the disks of dough on a lightly floured work surface and use a rolling pin to roll it out to about ¼ inch thick. Use the circular cookie cutter to cut out approximately twenty-four cookies and transfer them to the prepared trays. Repeat with the second disk of dough.

10. Bake for 10 minutes, or until the cookies are very lightly browned around the edges.

11. Remove the cookies from the oven and allow them to cool on the pan slightly before transferring them to wire racks to cool completely.

12. In a double boiler over medium heat, or a small heatproof bowl set over a pot of simmering water, melt the white chocolate chips. Remove from the heat and set aside.

13. Using your food processor or a large knife, finely chop the candy corn. Place it in a shallow bowl. Set aside.

14. Turn over twenty-four of the cooled cookies, bottom side up. Spoon about 1 teaspoon of melted chocolate on each one. Top with the remaining cookies and press down lightly to push the white chocolate to the outer edges of the sandwich cookie.

15. Roll the edges of the exposed white chocolate in the chopped candy corn and then place on wire racks until the chocolate has set. You can place the cookies in the refrigerator to speed up this process.

*H*alloween got me thinking about black cats and black cats got me thinking about black pepper and black pepper got me thinking about cookies. And well, I'm always thinking about chocolate. So that's the roundabout way these cookies came to be. I'm not exactly a linear thinker.

Chocolate Black Pepper Cat Cookies

2 cups all-purpose flour

½ cup dark cocoa

2 teaspoons baking powder

2 teaspoons black pepper

½ teaspoon salt

½ cup butter, room temperature

1 ¼ cups granulated sugar

1 large egg

1 teaspoon pure vanilla

1 cup dark chocolate chips

MAKES: **About 1 ½ dozen cookies**

YOU WILL NEED: **1 (11- x 17-inch) rimmed cookie sheet lined with parchment paper, 3- to 4-inch cat-shaped cookie cutter or cutter shape of your choice**

STORAGE: **These cookies will keep in an airtight container for up to 1 week.**

1. Preheat the oven to 350°F.

2. On a large piece of parchment paper, sift the flour, cocoa, baking powder, black pepper and salt. Set aside.

3. In a stand mixer fitted with a paddle attachment, cream the butter and sugar on high speed until light and fluffy. Scrape down the sides of the bowl.

4. Turn the mixer speed to medium and add the egg and vanilla. Beat to combine. Scrape down the sides of the bowl.

5. Turn the mixer speed to low and slowly add the dry ingredients. Beat until fully combined.

6. On a lightly floured work surface, use your rolling pin to roll the dough to about ¼ inch thick. Use your cookie cutter to cut out as many cookies as you can. Reroll the scraps and repeat until all the dough has been used.

7. Bake for 10 to 12 minutes, or until the cookies are firm around the edges.

8. Remove the cookies from the oven and allow them to cool slightly on the pan before transferring them to wire racks to cool completely.

9. In a double boiler over medium heat, or a small heatproof bowl set over a pot of simmering water, melt the chocolate chips. Remove from the heat.

10. Once the cookies have cooled, dip half of each cookie in the melted chocolate and then place it back on the tray until the chocolate has set. You can place the dipped cookies in the refrigerator to speed up the chocolate setting.

*M*oist but cakey, a subtle hint of pumpkin and the added crunch of pecans make this brownie one of my favorites. Some people switch up their wardrobes to work with the changing seasons. I find it more important to switch up my brownies.

Pumpkin Pecan Layered Brownies

PUMPKIN LAYER

1 cup cream cheese, full fat

½ cup canned pumpkin

1 large egg

¼ cup granulated sugar

1 teaspoon pumpkin pie spice

BROWNIES

2 cups dark chocolate chips

¾ cup butter

1 ½ cups all-purpose flour

½ cup dark cocoa

½ teaspoon salt

3 large eggs

1 cup granulated sugar

½ cup pecans, chopped

MAKES: 16 bars

YOU WILL NEED: 1 (9- x 9-inch) baking pan, buttered and lined with parchment paper

STORAGE: These brownies will keep in an airtight container for up to 1 week or in the freezer for 3 months.

1. Preheat the oven to 350°F.

2. For the pumpkin layer, in a stand mixer fitted with a paddle attachment, beat the cream cheese on high for several minutes. Scrape down the sides of the bowl and add the pumpkin, egg, sugar and pumpkin pie spice. Beat on medium speed until smooth. Pour the mixture into a small bowl and set aside. Give the mixer bowl and paddle a quick wash because you will need it again for the brownie batter.

3. For the brownies, in a double boiler over medium heat, or a small heatproof bowl set over simmering water, melt the chocolate and butter and whisk to combine. Remove from the heat and set aside.

4. On a large piece of parchment paper, sift the flour, cocoa and salt. Set aside.

5. In a stand mixer fitted with a paddle attachment, beat the eggs and sugar on high speed until very pale yellow. Turn the mixer speed to medium and carefully add the melted chocolate. Scrape down the sides of the bowl.

6. Turn the mixer speed to low and slowly add the dry ingredients. Scrape the sides of the bowl and beat again.

7. Pour half of the brownie batter into the prepared pan. Use a small offset spatula or the back of a spoon to spread it evenly. Top with the pumpkin layer and gently spread it across the bottom layer. Work slowly to avoid mixing the two layers together as best you can. Sprinkle the pecans over the pumpkin layer and then top with the remaining brownie batter, again using the offset spatula or spoon to help spread it evenly.

8. Bake for 30 minutes, or until a wooden skewer inserted in the center of the brownies comes out clean.

9. Remove the brownies from the oven and allow them to cool completely in the pan. Once cool, you can gently lift the brownie slab from the pan using the handles created by the parchment overhang and then cut it into sixteen pieces with a large knife.

*T*his is a simple and silly little add-on to your Halloween menu. They are perfect atop a cupcake or as standalone little treats that look really cute when clustered together on a platter like a little ghost flash mob.

Lil' Ghost Meringues

1 recipe Little Meringue Booties mix (page 94)

1 cup dark chocolate chips

MAKES: 4 dozen little ghosts

YOU WILL NEED: 2 (11- x 17-inch) rimmed cookie sheets lined with parchment paper, 14-inch piping bag fitted with a large plain tip, 10-inch piping bag fitted with a small plain tip

STORAGE: The meringues will keep in an airtight container for up to 1 week.

1. Preheat the oven to 225°F. Follow steps 1 and 2 for the Little Meringue Booties.

2. Fill your 14-inch piping bag fitted with a large plain tip with the meringue. Pipe a ghost onto the prepared cookie sheets by holding the bag upright with the tip pointing straight down. Apply pressure by squeezing the bag to release the meringue and create the base of the ghost. Gently start pulling up as you are squeezing to create the body of the ghost. Stop squeezing and pull up on the bag to create a little pointy top. Repeat, spacing the ghosts about 1 inch apart.

3. Refer back to the meringue recipe and follow step 4.

4. In a double boiler over medium heat, or a small heatproof bowl set over simmering water, melt the chocolate chips. Or melt the chocolate chips in your microwave by placing them in a small ceramic or glass bowl for 15 to 20 seconds, depending on the strength of your appliance.

5. Transfer the melted chocolate to your 10-inch piping bag fitted with a small plain tip. Carefully pipe two little eyes and a mouth on each ghost. Allow the meringues to sit for at least 1 hour for the chocolate to set.

*W*ho doesn't love food on a stick? Delicious and convenient.

Spicy Graham Caramel Apples

CRUMB MIXTURE

1 cup graham crumbs

1 tablespoon ground cinnamon

1 teaspoon ground nutmeg

½ teaspoon ground cloves

2 tablespoons granulated sugar

2 tablespoons butter, melted

CARAMEL APPLES

6 to 8 large apples (I like to use
    Granny Smith but you can pick
    your favorite)

2 cups light brown sugar

¼ cup water

¼ cup corn syrup, light or golden

½ teaspoon salt

2 tablespoons butter

2 tablespoons heavy cream

MAKES: 6 to 8 caramel apples

YOU WILL NEED: candy thermometer,
    2 (11- x 17-inch) rimmed cookie
    sheets lined with parchment
    paper, 6 to 8 Popsicle sticks

STORAGE: The apples will keep in
    an airtight container in the
    refrigerator for up to 1 week.

1. Preheat the oven to 350°F.

2. For the crumb mixture, in a medium bowl, combine the graham crumbs, spices, sugar and melted butter. Use a wooden spoon to stir until fully combined.

3. Spread the graham crumb mixture across one of the prepared cookie sheets and bake for 10 to 12 minutes, until lightly toasted. Remove from the oven and set aside to cool.

4. For the caramel apples, pierce the top of each apple in its center with a Popsicle stick. Set aside.

5. In a medium pot set over high heat, combine the brown sugar, water, corn syrup and salt. Clip the candy thermometer to the side of the pot.

6. Using a whisk, stir the mixture constantly until the temperature reaches 280°F. Use a wet pastry brush to wash off any sugar crystals that form on the sides of the pot.

7. Remove from the heat and stir in the butter and cream. Be careful as you do this as the caramel may bubble up and spit when these are first added.

8. Holding an apple by its stick, dip it in the caramel and slowly turn it to evenly coat. Lift the apple from the caramel and hold it over the pot until it stops dripping.

9. Roll the coated apple across the toasted graham crumbs and then give the bottom a little stamp to coat it too. Set it aside on the other prepared tray until the caramel has fully set, about 15 minutes. Repeat with the remaining apples.

Thanksgiving

Thanksgiving is like Christmas without the pressure and stress of shopping for presents. So, Thanksgiving, for this I thank you. Thank you for just letting me focus on the important stuff like juicy turkey, my mum's bread stuffing, creamy spinach (everyone's favorite . . . I swear!), mashed potatoes, gravy, pumpkin pie, whipped cream, family, friends, football (just kidding, I don't give a hoot about football), mismatched chairs around a very long table, parades, a holiday weekend, puffy vests, crisp air and the smell of chimney smoke.

*I*f fall were a layer cake, this would be it. If I were a layer cake, I don't know what flavor I'd be. But I'd definitely be at least eight layers. Paul would confirm that all my quirks just couldn't possibly fit in four layers.

Apple Spice Layer Cake
with Brown Sugar Maple Frosting

2 ½ cups pastry flour

1 ½ teaspoons ground cinnamon

1 ½ teaspoons baking soda

¾ teaspoon baking powder

½ teaspoon salt

1 cup light brown sugar

½ cup granulated sugar

1 cup vegetable oil

3 large eggs

1 large apple, peeled and grated
(Granny Smith or Ambrosia are
my favorites)

1 cup apple sauce

1 ½ teaspoons pure vanilla

FINISHING TOUCHES

1 recipe Brown Sugar Maple
Frosting (page 124)

MAKES: 1 (8-inch) four-layer cake,
serves 8 to 12

YOU WILL NEED: 2 (8-inch) circular
cake pans, buttered and floured,
rotating cake stand, large
serrated knife

1. Preheat the oven to 350°F.

2. On a large piece of parchment paper, sift the flour, cinnamon, baking soda, baking powder and salt. Set aside.

3. In a large mixing bowl, whisk together the sugars and oil. Add the eggs and continue whisking until the mixture becomes paler. Add the grated apple, apple sauce and vanilla and whisk to combine.

4. Sprinkle the dry ingredients over the batter and use a rubber spatula or wooden spoon to blend.

5. Divide the batter evenly between the two prepared pans. Bake for 30 to 35 minutes until the cake springs back when lightly touched and a wooden skewer inserted in the center of a cake comes out clean.

6. Remove the cakes from the oven and allow them to cool slightly in the pans before inverting them onto wire racks to cool completely. You may need to run a sharp knife around the edges of the pan if the cakes do not easily fall when first inverted.

7. Meanwhile, prepare the Brown Sugar Maple Frosting.

8. Transfer the cakes to a rotating cake stand and use a large serrated knife to cut each cake in half on the horizontal to create four layers.

9. Place your first layer on a cake stand or plate. Use a large offset spatula to spread a generous helping of frosting across the cake layer. Place the second layer on top and repeat the process until all the layers are frosted.

10. Continue to use your offset spatula to ice the top and sides of the cake. There's no need to try to make it super smooth as this particular frosting looks great with a few ups, downs and swirl-arounds!

*T*his tart is as delicious as it is beautiful—and a wonderful excuse to use up all the apples that will be falling from the trees at this time of year. Granny Smith or Gala work great, but the choice is yours. Don't choose too large an apple, though, as the slices will be too big to fit nicely in the tart shell.

Apple Custard Tart

One 9-inch Simply Tart Dough shell
(page 36)

4 medium-sized tart apples

½ cup light brown sugar

1 teaspoon ground cinnamon

½ teaspoon ground cardamom

½ cup granulated sugar

2 tablespoons all-purpose flour

½ teaspoon salt

½ cup heavy cream

2 large eggs

MAKES: 1 (9-inch) tart, serves 8 to 10

YOU WILL NEED: 1 (9-inch) tart pan,
1 (11- x 17-inch) rimmed cookie
sheet lined with parchment paper

1. Prepare a 9-inch tart shell of Simply Tart Dough through step 8. Set aside.

2. Preheat the oven to 350°F.

3. Prepare the apples by using a small paring knife to peel and cut them in quarters. Once quartered, trim any core from each section. Cut each quarter into ⅛-inch slices. It is best if you can keep your slices uniform in shape and size so they sit nicely in the tart shell.

4. Place the apple slices in a large bowl. Add the brown sugar, cinnamon and cardamom. Use your hands to gently lift the apple slices to coat them in the sugar mixture, taking care not to break them. Set aside. Arrange the apple slices in concentric circles in the tart shell.

5. Bake for 15 to 20 minutes, or just until the apples start to color. Remove the tart from the oven and allow it to cool slightly.

6. Meanwhile, in another bowl, whisk together the granulated sugar, flour, salt, cream and eggs.

7. Place the tart pan on the prepared cookie sheet before pouring the custard mixture carefully over the top of the apples. Pour slowly to allow the custard to work its way under the apples. If you pour too quickly it may spill over the edges of the tart shell, making the tart difficult to remove from the pan once it's baked.

8. Return the tart to the oven and bake for another 30 to 40 minutes, or until the custard has set and your tart shell is a light golden brown.

9. Remove the tart from the oven and allow it to cool in the pan on a wire rack for about 1 hour before removing from the tart pan and slicing.

he smell of this loaf baking will attract people from miles around. So think long and hard before you make it, just in case you don't feel like having anyone over that day.

Pumpkin Pecan Loaf

2 cups all-purpose flour

2 teaspoons baking powder

2 teaspoons baking soda

1 tablespoon plus ½ teaspoon ground cinnamon

1 teaspoon ground nutmeg

1 teaspoon ground ginger

½ teaspoon salt

3 large eggs

1 ¼ cups granulated sugar

1 cup canned pumpkin

1 cup vegetable oil

2 teaspoons pure vanilla

⅓ cup dark brown sugar

3 tablespoons butter, melted

½ cup pecans

MAKES: 2 (8-inch) loaves, 8 to 10 slices per loaf

YOU WILL NEED: 2 (8-inch) loaf pans, buttered and floured

STORAGE: This loaf will keep in an airtight container for up to 1 week or in the freezer for up to 3 months.

1. Preheat the oven to 350°F.

2. On a large piece of parchment paper, sift together the flour, baking powder, baking soda, 1 tablespoon of the cinnamon, the nutmeg, ginger and salt. Set aside.

3. In a stand mixer fitted with a paddle attachment, beat the eggs on medium speed until pale. Add the granulated sugar, pumpkin, oil and vanilla and mix to combine.

4. Turn the mixer speed to low and slowly add the dry ingredients. Mix until just combined. Scrape down the sides of the bowl and give the mixer a couple more turns.

5. Divide the batter evenly between the two prepared loaf pans. Use a spatula to spread it smoothly across the top.

6. In a small bowl, combine the melted butter, the remaining ½ teaspoon cinnamon and brown sugar and whisk to create a paste.

7. Spoon the brown sugar mixture down the center of each loaf and sprinkle with the pecans.

8. Bake for 35 to 40 minutes, or until a wooden skewer inserted in the center of the loaf comes out clean.

9. Remove the loaves from the oven and allow them to cool slightly in the pans before transferring them to wire racks to cool completely. Once they are cool, use a serrated knife to cut them and serve to all those people who have now gathered in your kitchen.

Sprinkling the sugar and icing the veins on the cookies are optional. These cookies are just as yummy as they come, alongside a nice cup of tea.

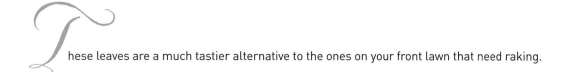

These leaves are a much tastier alternative to the ones on your front lawn that need raking.

Falling Leaves Spice Cookies

2 ¼ cups all-purpose flour

2 teaspoons baking powder

1 teaspoon ground cinnamon

½ teaspoon ground ginger

¼ teaspoon ground nutmeg

¼ teaspoon ground cloves

½ teaspoon salt

½ cup butter, room temperature

½ cup light brown sugar

½ cup granulated sugar

1 large egg

1 teaspoon pure vanilla

FINISHING TOUCHES

Coarse sanding sugar in fall colors
   (orange, yellow and green)

1 recipe Royal Icing (page 122)

MAKES: **2 dozen cookies**

YOU WILL NEED: 2 (11- x 17-inch)
   rimmed cookie sheets lined with
   parchment paper, 2- to 3-inch
   leaf cookie cutters, 10-inch
   piping bag fitted with a small
   plain tip

STORAGE: **These cookies will keep
   in an airtight container for up to
   2 weeks and in the freezer for up
   to 3 months.**

1. Preheat the oven to 350°F.

2. On a large piece of parchment paper, sift the flour, baking powder, cinnamon, ginger, nutmeg, cloves and salt. Set aside.

3. In a stand mixer fitted with a paddle attachment, cream the butter and both sugars until light and fluffy. Scrape down the sides of the bowl. Add the egg and vanilla and mix to combine. Scrape down the sides of the bowl again.

4. Turn the mixer speed to low and slowly add the dry ingredients, mixing until fully combined.

5. Turn the dough out onto a lightly floured work surface. Use your rolling pin to roll the dough to about ¼ inch thick.

6. Use the cookie cutters to cut out as many cookies as you can. Carefully transfer them to the prepared cookie sheets, about ½ inch apart. Combine the dough scraps, reroll and repeat until all the dough has been used.

7. Sprinkle the top of the unbaked cookies with the sanding sugar, to mime the shades of fall leaves.

8. Bake for 13 to 15 minutes, or until the cookies are lightly browned around the edges.

9. Remove the cookies from the oven and allow them to cool slightly before transferring them to wire racks to cool completely.

10. Meanwhile, make a bowl of Royal Icing and follow the instructions to tint it brown (page 55).

11. Once the cookies have cooled, fill your 10-inch piping bag with icing and carefully ice the veins of a leaf on each cookie. Place the cookies back on the wire rack for about 30 minutes to allow the icing to set.

I'm warning you, you have to be a fan of raisins to like this cookie. If you aren't, might I suggest the Cookie Jar Cookies (page 109)? If you are a fan of raisins, then let's proceed, shall we?

Soft Raisin Cookies

1 cup pure unsweetened apple juice

1 ½ cups sultana raisins (they are my favorite but you can substitute with your own favorite)

1 teaspoon ground cinnamon

½ teaspoon ground nutmeg

½ teaspoon ground ginger

¼ teaspoon ground cloves

2 cups all-purpose flour

1 teaspoon baking soda

½ teaspoon salt

⅓ cup butter, room temperature

1 cup granulated sugar

1 large egg

MAKES: **2 dozen cookies**

YOU WILL NEED: **2 (11- x 17-inch) rimmed cookie sheets lined with parchment paper, medium ice cream scoop**

STORAGE: **These cookies will keep in an airtight container for up to 1 week or in the freezer for up to 3 months.**

1. Preheat the oven to 350°F.

2. In a small pot over high heat, combine the apple juice, raisins, cinnamon, nutmeg, ginger and cloves. Boil gently for 12 to 15 minutes, until the liquid has boiled off just to the top of the raisins.

3. On a large piece of parchment paper, sift the flour, baking soda and salt. Set aside.

4. In a stand mixer fitted with a paddle attachment, cream the butter and sugar until light and fluffy. Scrape down the sides of the bowl. Add the egg and mix to combine. Scrape down the sides of the bowl again.

5. With the mixer running on low speed, add the dry ingredients, cooled raisins and any remaining liquid. Turn the mixer speed to medium and mix until well combined.

6. Use your ice cream scoop to drop twenty-four evenly sized balls of dough on the prepared cookie sheets, about 1 ½ inches apart.

7. Bake for 12 to 15 minutes, or until the cookies are just firm around the edges and spring back in the center when touched.

8. Remove the cookies from the oven and allow them to cool slightly before transferring them to wire racks to cool completely.

I want to tell you how delicious this bar is, but it is rude to talk with your mouth full. So just imagine I'm enthusiastically holding two thumbs up.

Pumpkin Chocolate Cheesecake Bar

½ cup plus 2 tablespoons butter

2 cups chocolate crumbs

Two 8-ounce packages cream cheese, full fat

1 large egg

¾ cup canned pumpkin

¾ cup granulated sugar

1 teaspoon ground ginger

1 teaspoon pumpkin pie spice

½ teaspoon salt

1 cup dark chocolate chips

MAKES: 16 bars

YOU WILL NEED: 1 (9- x 9-inch) baking pan buttered and lined with parchment

STORAGE: These bars will keep in an airtight container in your refrigerator for up to 1 week or in your freezer for up to 3 months.

1. Preheat the oven to 350°F.

2. In a small pot over medium heat, melt ½ cup of the butter. Pour it over the chocolate crumbs in a medium mixing bowl and use a wooden spoon or spatula to combine and evenly coat the crumbs.

3. Press the chocolate crumbs firmly into the prepared pan to create the base. Bake for 10 minutes. Remove from the oven and set aside.

4. In a stand mixer fitted with a paddle attachment, cream the cream cheese until light and fluffy. Scrape down the sides of the bowl and add the egg, pumpkin, sugar, spices and salt. Beat again to combine until smooth. Scrape down the sides of the bowl at least once during this process.

5. Pour the batter over the chocolate base and return it to the oven to bake for another 30 minutes, or until the filling is firm to the touch.

6. Remove the bars from the oven and allow it to cool completely.

7. Meanwhile, in a double boiler over medium heat, or a small heatproof bowl set over simmering water, melt the chocolate chips and the remaining 2 tablespoons butter. Pour the melted chocolate over the top of the cooled pumpkin layer and use a small offset spatula to help spread it evenly. You can give the pan a light tap on the edge of the counter to help settle the chocolate in one smooth layer.

8. Place the pan in the refrigerator for about 30 minutes so the chocolate sets up.

9. Once the chocolate has set, run a knife along the edges of the pan that aren't lined with parchment paper. Use the parchment handles to carefully lift the slab from the pan in one piece. Then use a large chef's knife to cut the slab into 16 bars.

utterscotch, if Paul hadn't snatched me up first, I totally would have married you. Is it wrong for me to assume you would have asked?

Butterscotch Walnut Pie

1 recipe Everyday Pastry pie shell
   (page 141)

½ cup butterscotch chips

⅔ cup corn syrup, light or golden

¼ cup dark brown sugar

¼ cup butter

2 large eggs

1 ½ teaspoons pure vanilla

1 ½ cups walnuts, whole or pieces

MAKES: 1 (9-inch) pie, 8 to 10 slices

YOU WILL NEED: 1 (9-inch) glass
   pie dish

1. Preheat the oven to 350°F.

2. Make a batch of Everyday Pastry. Take one half of the chilled dough and place it on a lightly floured work surface. Use your rolling pin to roll the dough to about ⅛ inch thick and 11 inches in diameter. Carefully fold the dough into quarters and gently transfer it to the pie dish. Unfold and press the dough lightly into place. Trim the dough with a knife or scissors to leave about a 1-inch overhang. Roll and tuck the 1-inch overhang back under the edges of the pie shell. Use your index finger of your right hand to push the dough out toward the edge of the pie shell and your index finger and thumb of your left hand to pinch it into a point each time you do. Continue until you have circled the pie shell. Set aside.

3. In a medium pot set over medium heat, combine the butterscotch chips with the corn syrup, brown sugar and butter. Use a heatproof rubber spatula or wooden spoon to stir until the butterscotch chips have completely melted. Set aside to cool.

4. In a medium mixing bowl, whisk together the eggs and vanilla. Pour the cooled butterscotch mixture into the eggs and whisk again to combine. Set aside.

5. Sprinkle the walnuts evenly across the bottom of the prepared pie shell. Pour the butterscotch filling over the walnuts and bake the pie for approximately 1 hour, or until the center of the pie puffs up and cracks. When you jiggle the pie the center should appear quite firm.

6. Remove the pie from the oven. Place the dish on a wire rack and allow the pie to cool completely before slicing.

*T*he perfect dessert for a damp fall evening when that chill in the air tells you winter is on its way. If you time it right, you will be pulling this dish hot from the oven just as you finish your supper. Scoop up a bowlful and top it with a big dollop of spiced whipped cream. A couple of mouthfuls in and I promise you will have forgotten all about the colder months ahead.

Pear Cranberry Crumble with Cardamom Whip

6 large pears (Bosc or Bartlett), peeled, cored and cut in ½-inch cubes

1 ½ cups fresh cranberries

½ cup dark brown sugar

¼ cup water

2 tablespoons lemon juice

1 tablespoon ground cinnamon

Zest of 1 lemon

CRUMBLE TOPPING

1 ½ cups all-purpose flour

¾ cup dark brown sugar

½ cup butter, chilled and cut into 1-inch pieces

CARDAMOM WHIP

2 cups heavy cream

¼ cup granulated sugar

1 teaspoon ground cardamom

2 teaspoons pure vanilla

MAKES: 1 (9- x 13-inch) crumble, serves 8

YOU WILL NEED: 1 (9- x 13-inch) rectangular baking dish, buttered

1. Preheat the oven to 350°F.

2. In a large bowl, combine the chopped pears, cranberries, ½ cup sugar, water, lemon juice, cinnamon and lemon zest. Use a wooden spoon or your hands to stir and coat all the fruit with the brown sugar mixture. Place the coated fruit in the prepared baking dish.

3. For the crumble topping, in a medium bowl, combine the flour and ¾ cup sugar. Use a pastry cutter or two knives to cut in the chilled butter until large, buttery crumbs are formed. Sprinkle the crumble topping across the top of the fruit.

4. Bake for 50 to 60 minutes, or until the juice from the fruit is bubbling up through the crumble topping.

5. Meanwhile, prepare the Cardamom Whip. In a stand mixer fitted with a whisk attachment, whip the cream, sugar, cardamom and vanilla on high speed until soft peaks form. Be careful not to look away, as a minute too long and you will be spreading cardamom butter on your toast tomorrow morning.

6. Remove the crumble from the oven and prepare to serve with spoonfuls of the Cardamom Whip.

I'm really not sure who started the tradition of putting marshmallows on top of sweet potatoes for Thanksgiving dinner but they were clearly onto something. They were just a little confused about the point in the meal you were to serve this dish. Not to worry. I sorted it all out. Now it makes perfect sense!

Sweet Potato Marshmallow Pie

2 cups sweet potato, baked, peeled and mashed (about 2 large sweet potatoes)

1 recipe Everyday Pastry pie shell (page 141)

2 large eggs

300 ml can condensed milk

1 ½ cups granulated sugar

1 teaspoon ground cinnamon

½ teaspoon ground nutmeg

½ teaspoon salt

1 recipe Vanilla Marshmallow (page 54)

MAKES: 1 (9-inch) pie, 8 to 10 slices

YOU WILL NEED: 1 (9-inch) glass pie dish, candy thermometer, kitchen blowtorch

1. Preheat the oven to 375°F.

2. Poke several holes in each sweet potato and place them in a baking dish. Bake for approximately 1 hour, or until the sweet potatoes are soft to the touch when you give them a light squeeze. Remove the sweet potatoes from the oven and set them aside until they are cool enough to remove the skins with a small paring knife. The skins should peel off very easily. Place the peeled sweet potato flesh in a medium bowl and mash it with the back of a fork until smooth. Set aside.

3. Turn down the oven temperature to 350°F.

4. Make a batch of Everyday Pastry. Take one half of the chilled dough and place it on a lightly floured work surface. Use a rolling pin to roll the dough to about ⅛ inch thick and 11 inches in diameter. Carefully fold the dough into quarters and gently transfer it to the pie dish. Unfold the pastry and press it lightly into place. Trim the dough with a knife or scissors to leave about a 1-inch overhang. Roll and tuck the 1-inch overhang back under the edges of the pie shell. Use your index finger of your right hand to push the dough out toward the edge of the pie shell and your index finger and thumb of your left hand to pinch it into a point each time you do. Continue until you have circled the pie shell. Set aside.

5. In another bowl, whisk together the eggs, condensed milk, sugar, cinnamon, nutmeg and salt. Add the egg mixture to the sweet potato and whisk until fully combined.

6. Pour the sweet potato filling into the prepared pie shell and bake for 60 to 75 minutes, or until the center of the pie is set and the shell is a lovely golden brown.

7. Remove the pie from the oven and allow it to cool completely on a wire rack before topping with the marshmallow.

8. Prepare a batch of Vanilla Marshmallow as directed in Coconut Marshmallow Bunnies (page 54) through step 4. The marshmallow will begin to set up almost immediately, so don't start this step too soon.

9. Spoon the prepared marshmallow over the top of the cooled pie and use the back of the spoon to make gentle swirls on top. It is best to leave the pie to sit for at least 2 hours to let it set up fully prior to browning and slicing. Once the marshmallow has fully set you can use your kitchen blowtorch to carefully brown and toast it.

Hanukkah

An education is a wonderful thing, made even more so when it's crazy delicious. Every year around Hanukkah, Butter gets lots of requests for our shaped cookies. We ice up little dreidels, candlelit menorahs and the Star of David in shades of blue, gold and white, but I am afraid to admit that that was as deep as my knowledge in the Hanukkah baked goods department went. I was curious to learn more, so I started asking questions, or rather one very important question: "What's your favorite treat at Hanukkah?" My teachers were kind and more than happy to help bring me up to speed and I literally devoured every one of my lessons. Can't blame the dog for eating my homework this time. It was me, all me.

My daughter's friends Max and Brad proved to be excellent resources, as did Max's mom, who sent over some pretty fine baking to sample! But in the end I set out to create the items that really spoke to me and the idea of jelly doughnuts, rugelach and challah wasn't just speaking to me, it was tap dancing while screaming my name through a bull horn. The only question I have now is, "How do you feel about celebrating Hanukkah a little more often? Say, like every Tuesday?"

I perfected this recipe on my birthday last year and it was the greatest gift of all time! It's hard to describe the sense of pride and accomplishment I felt as I rolled these fluffy little pillows in sugar. My chest swelled at the sight of all my little doughnut children. Then I ate them. Does that make me a lousy mother?

Sufganiyot

(also known as the jelly doughnut)

2 packages instant yeast

¼ cup warm water

3 ¾ cups all-purpose flour

½ cup granulated sugar

¼ cup butter, room temperature

½ teaspoon salt

3 egg yolks

1 cup buttermilk

1 teaspoon pure vanilla

FINISHING TOUCHES

½ cup raspberry jam (or jam of your choosing)

1 cup granulated sugar

MAKES: 30 little doughnuts (you can always use a larger cutter if you want a more traditionally sized jelly doughnut)

YOU WILL NEED: electric deep-fryer, 1 (11- x 17-inch) rimmed cookie sheet lined with parchment paper, 1 (11- x 17-inch) rimmed cookie sheet lined with paper towel, 2-inch circular cutter, 10-inch piping bag fitted with a plain tip

1. In a small bowl, sprinkle the yeast into the warm water. Set aside to bloom.

2. In a stand mixer fitted with a paddle attachment, combine the flour, sugar, butter and salt. Beat on medium speed until the butter is evenly distributed throughout the flour.

3. In a liquid measuring cup, whisk together the egg yolks, buttermilk and vanilla and pour into the bowl of the mixer with the dry ingredients. Then add the yeast with its water. Turn the mixer speed to low and continue to beat until well combined.

4. Turn off the mixer and replace the paddle attachment with a dough hook. Turn the mixer speed to high and allow the dough hook to knead the dough for about 5 minutes, until the dough is shiny, smooth and elastic.

5. Place the dough in a lightly oiled bowl, cover loosely with plastic wrap and leave it in a warm, draft-free spot. Allow the dough to rise for 30 to 45 minutes. You aren't looking for it to double in size but rather just to gain a little volume and air.

6. Turn the dough out onto a lightly floured work surface and use a rolling pin to gently release some of the air the yeast has created by rolling it over the dough a few times. Let the dough rest for about 10 minutes and then roll it to about ¼ inch thick. Use your circular cutter to cut out as many doughnuts as you can and place them on the tray lined with parchment paper. Reroll and gently knead the scraps into a smooth ball. Repeat.

7. Loosely cover the tray in plastic wrap and allow it to sit in a warm, draft-free spot until the doughnuts have risen to nearly double in size.

8. Fill the piping bag fitted with a plain tip with the raspberry jam. Twist the bag to close it and set aside.

9. Fill a large shallow bowl with the sugar. Set aside.

10. Follow the instructions for preparing your deep-fryer for use. I like to use a vegetable shortening to fry the doughnuts. Set the temperature gauge to 350°F.

11. Once the oil has reached the desired temperature, very gently place a couple of doughnuts in the oil. Don't overcrowd them and don't just drop them in. You don't want to get splashed with hot oil. Allow the doughnuts to cook for approximately 1 minute per side. Use a metal slotted spoon to help turn the doughnuts over at the halfway point. Once cooked, use the slotted spoon to carefully lift the doughnuts from the hot oil and transfer them to the bowl of sugar. Use another spoon to sprinkle the sugar over the top and sides of the doughnut and then gently lift it from the sugar and place it on the tray lined with paper towel. Repeat with the balance of the doughnuts.

12. When the doughnuts are cool enough to handle, use the pastry tip on your filled piping bag to pierce one end. Gently squeeze the bag to fill the doughnut with jam. Repeat with the balance of the doughnuts.

You can always deep-fry without the use of an electric deep-fryer by filling a large, deep, heavy-bottomed pot with vegetable oil or shortening and using your candy thermometer to establish the correct temperature when heating the oil, but this method does prove really challenging when trying to keep the temperature consistent. I much prefer the cleanliness, safety and convenience of a self-contained appliance.

I wondered what would happen if I melded the idea of a Butter cinnamon bun and challah loaf. Oh, believe me, people . . . good things happened. This bread is wonderful warm from the oven or lightly toasted with butter, but in French toast it has found its true calling. So you might want to say "hola" to this challah all the time.

Apple-Stuffed Challah

CHALLAH

1 package instant yeast

¼ cup warm water

4 cups all-purpose flour

¼ cup granulated sugar

2 tablespoons butter

1 teaspoon salt

2 tablespoons liquid honey

2 large eggs

2 egg yolks

2 tablespoons vegetable oil

¾ cup water

APPLE STUFFING

2 apples, peeled, cored and cut into
   ½-inch cubes (something tart,
   like a Granny Smith, works well)

2 tablespoons dark brown sugar

1 tablespoon liquid honey

1 teaspoon ground cinnamon

FINISHING TOUCHES

1 large egg

2 tablespoons water

Coarse sanding sugar

1. For the challah, in a small bowl, sprinkle the yeast into the warm water. Set aside to bloom.

2. In a stand mixer fitted with a paddle attachment, combine the flour, sugar, butter and salt on medium speed. Continue to beat until the butter has been distributed throughout the flour.

3. In a liquid measuring cup, whisk together the honey, eggs, egg yolks, oil and water. Turn the mixer speed to low and add the liquid ingredients to the dry ingredients. Add the yeast with its water and continue beating until well combined.

4. Stop the mixer and change the paddle attachment to a dough hook.

5. Turn the mixer speed to high and let the dough hook knead the dough for at least 5 minutes, until it is shiny, smooth and elastic.

6. Place the dough in a lightly oiled bowl and cover loosely with plastic wrap. Place the bowl in a warm, draft-free spot and allow the dough to rise until it has doubled in size, about 90 minutes.

7. Meanwhile, prepare the apple stuffing. In a medium bowl, combine the chopped apple, brown sugar, honey and cinnamon. Use a wooden spoon to stir and coat all the apples. Set aside.

8. Once the dough has fully risen, remove the plastic wrap and punch down the dough to release the air produced by the yeast. Turn the dough out onto a lightly floured work surface and allow it to rest for about 10 minutes.   ☞

MAKES: 1 loaf, 8 to 10 slices

YOU WILL NEED: 1 (11- x 17-inch) rimmed cookie sheet lined with parchment paper

STORAGE: Apple challah can be kept well wrapped or in an airtight container for several days. Especially because you can toast it.

9. Use a knife to divide the dough into three equal pieces. Use your rolling pin to roll each piece into a rectangle approximately 14 inches long and 6 inches wide. Place one-third of the apple filling down the center of a piece of dough. Pull one side of the dough over the filling and pinch to seal it closed on the other side and at the top and bottom. This will create a filled log of dough. Repeat with the other two pieces of dough.

10. Lay one of the logs vertically along the center of the prepared cookie sheet. Lay a second log across the middle of it, with the ends of the log pointing at 10 o' clock and 4 o' clock. Then lay the third log across the middle on top, with the ends pointing at 2 o' clock and 8 o' clock. Braid one side of the loaf from the middle down and then tuck the ends under. Turn the cookie sheet and repeat with the other side.

11. In a small bowl, combine the egg and water and use your pastry brush to generously coat the top and sides of the loaf with the egg wash. Sprinkle with the sanding sugar.

12. Cover the loaf loosely with a sheet of plastic wrap and set in a warm, draft-free place to rise again until it has nearly doubled in size, about 90 minutes.

13. Preheat the oven to 350°F.

14. Bake the loaf for 30 to 40 minutes, or until it is a lovely golden brown and a wooden skewer inserted in the center comes out clean.

15. Remove from the oven and allow the loaf to cool for at least 20 minutes on the cookie sheet before transferring to a cutting board and slicing.

*T*raditional rugelach is filled with jam, fruit and nuts, but chocolate and hazelnut seemed just a smidge more celebratory to me. It also provided me with another excuse to spread Nutella on something. These little crescent-shaped cookies fall under the more-ish category of baking. You eat one and you have to have more.

Chocolate Hazelnut Rugelach

1 ½ cups pastry flour

½ teaspoon baking soda

½ teaspoon salt

½ cup cream cheese, full fat

½ cup butter, room temperature

½ cup granulated sugar

1 cup Nutella

½ cup hazelnuts

FINISHING TOUCHES

1 large egg

1 tablespoon water

Course sanding sugar

MAKES: **2 dozen cookies**

YOU WILL NEED: **2 (11- x 17-inch) rimmed cookie sheets lined with parchment paper**

STORAGE: **These cookies will keep in an airtight container for up to 1 week or in the freezer for up to 3 months.**

1. On a large piece of parchment paper, sift the flour, baking soda and salt. Set aside.

2. In a stand mixer fitted with a paddle attachment, cream the cream cheese and butter on high speed until well blended. Scrape down the sides of the bowl. Add the sugar and continue to beat until light and fluffy. Scrape down the sides of the bowl.

3. Turn the mixer speed to low and slowly add the dry ingredients. Continue to beat until well combined.

4. Divide the dough in two. Wrap each piece in plastic wrap and chill in the refrigerator for at least 2 hours.

5. Preheat the oven to 350°F.

6. Place the Nutella in a small bowl and use a spoon to give it a good stir to help loosen it up. This will make it easier to spread across the tender dough.

7. Use a large chef's knife to chop the hazelnuts. Set aside.

8. Place a chilled piece of dough on a lightly floured work surface and use a rolling pin to roll it into a circle about 9 inches in diameter.

9. Use a small offset spatula to carefully spread the Nutella across the dough. The dough is very tender, so work carefully to avoid it tearing it. If it does tear, not to worry, just press it back together.

10. Sprinkle half of the chopped hazelnuts over the top of the Nutella.

11. Use the large chef's knife to cut the dough into quarters and then each quarter into thirds, just like if you were cutting a pie.

12. Start at the wide end of a piece of dough and roll it toward the point. Bend the two ends in slightly to create a crescent shape and then place it on a prepared tray.

13. Repeat with the balance of the dough.

14. Combine the egg and water in a small bowl and whisk them together. Use your pastry brush to lightly coat the top and sides of each cookie. Sprinkle generously with the sanding sugar.

15. Bake for approximately 15 minutes, or until the cookies have puffed up and are a lovely golden brown. Remove the cookies from the oven and transfer them to wire racks to cool.

Christmas

One of my strongest memories of Christmas, and clearly a defining moment in my life, would be the day, every year, that the cookies arrived by Greyhound bus. My Italian grandparents on my dad's side lived out of town. They came to visit several times a year, but rarely at Christmas. I imagine the roads would have been pretty icy in December (as would my mum had my grandparents shown up). But in their place would arrive a large brown box, carefully taped shut and bearing our family name and address in my grandma's familiar script. Some years my dad picked the box up on his way home from work, and some years, if you were lucky, you got to go with him to the bus station to retrieve it. Inside it held a wrapped present for each of us, always bound with a metallic stretchy ribbon that snapped over two of the corners. But the real gifts were tucked inside a bunch of old coffee tins, for this is how my grandma would package the cookies. A huge assortment of Italian Christmas cookies, a different kind in every tin. I loved that moment. Peeling back the plastic lids on each one, more reassured than surprised by its content. Always delighted when I found the Pizelle, a fragile waffle cookie, paper-thin and tasting faintly of anise. I don't think it was the actual cookies that left the impression but rather the luxury of having so many to choose from. It was decadent and special. It was Christmas.

*O*nce in a while, an occasion calls for something a little extra special. I'd say this cake fits the bill. It might seem a little finicky but it's worth the effort in the end and you will love how everyone goes "Oooohh" and "Aaahhh" when you bring it to the table.

Chocolate Gingerbread Genoise
(Fancypants Cake)

1 cup pastry flour

½ cup dark cocoa

6 large eggs, lightly beaten

1 ¼ cups granulated sugar

1 teaspoon cream of tartar

¼ cup butter, melted and cooled

FINISHING TOUCHES

1 recipe Gingerbread Italian Butter
    Cream (page 118)

1 recipe Chocolate Ganache
    (page 126)

MAKES: 1 (4- x 11-inch) four-layer
    cake, 10 to 12 pieces

YOU WILL NEED: 1 (11- x 17-inch)
    rimmed cookie sheet lined with
    parchment paper, candy
    thermometer

1. Preheat the oven to 350°F.

2. On a large piece of parchment paper, sift the flour and cocoa and set aside.

3. In a double boiler over medium heat, or a heatproof bowl set over simmering water, whisk together the eggs and sugar. Clip your candy thermometer to the side of the pot and warm the eggs and sugar until they reach 100°F. This will help add volume when you are whipping the egg mixture.

4. Transfer the egg mixture to the bowl of a stand mixer fitted with a whisk attachment. Whip the eggs and sugar until they are frothy and then add the cream of tartar. Continue mixing until the egg mixture has tripled in volume and is a pale creamy color. This should take about 10 minutes.

5. Remove the bowl from the mixer and use a spatula to very gently fold in the dry ingredients.

6. Slowly pour the melted butter around the edges of the batter and then continue to fold until it is fully incorporated.

7. Gently pour the batter onto the prepared tray, using the back of the spatula to spread it evenly.

8. Bake for 10 to 12 minutes, or until the center of the cake springs back when lightly touched.

9. Remove the cake from the oven and allow it to cool completely in the pan.

10. Prepare the Gingerbread Italian Butter Cream.

11. Once the cake has cooled, cut it into four equal pieces, approximately 4 × 11 inches each. Place the bottom layer of the cake on a wire rack. Using a large offset spatula, spread this layer with the butter cream. Repeat with the next two layers. Add the fourth layer on top and coat the entire exterior of the cake as evenly and smoothly as possible with the balance of the butter cream. Place the cake on the wire rack in the refrigerator for at least 1 hour.

12. Prepare the Chocolate Ganache.

13. Once the butter cream has set, remove the cake from the refrigerator and place the wire rack over a cookie sheet. This is to catch the drips when you are glazing the cake with the chocolate ganache.

14. Pour half the chocolate ganache down the middle of the cake lengthwise and allow it to start running down the sides. Use your offset spatula to work quickly to evenly coat the sides and top of the cake. Once the cake has been covered you can give the wire rack a couple of light taps on the tray to help the ganache settle smoothly. Place the cake back in the refrigerator for about 20 minutes, or until the ganache has set up.

Remove the cake from the refrigerator and repeat step 13 with the balance of the ganache. Once the final coating of ganache has set, the cake can be carefully transported using a large metal spatula to a cake board or serving platter.

*T*hese are one of my favorite Christmas treats—and they couldn't be easier to make. They are quite light, not too sweet and just the right size to leave room in my tummy for all the other holiday goodies I want to sample. Thank you, little cookies, for being so considerate of my wants and desires at this crazy time of year.

Holiday Gems

1 ¼ cups all-purpose flour

1 teaspoon baking powder

½ teaspoon anise seeds

½ teaspoon salt

¼ cup butter, room temperature

½ cup granulated sugar

1 large egg

1 egg yolk

¼ cup candied red and green cherries, chopped

¼ cup candied citrus peel

Zest of 1 orange

½ cup coarse sanding sugar, for rolling and coating

MAKES: **2 dozen cookies**

YOU WILL NEED: **1 (11- x 17-inch) rimmed cookie sheet lined with parchment paper, small ice cream scoop**

STORAGE: **These little gems will keep nicely in an airtight container for 1 week or in the freezer for up to 3 months.**

1. Preheat the oven to 350°F.

2. On a large piece of parchment paper, sift together the flour, baking powder, anise and salt. Set aside.

3. In a large stand mixer fitted with a paddle attachment, cream the butter and sugar on medium-high speed until light and fluffy. Using a spatula, scrape down the sides of the bowl. Add the egg and then the egg yolk, making sure to scrape down the sides of the bowl after each addition.

4. Turn the mixer speed to low, add the dry ingredients and mix to combine. Add the candied fruit and the orange zest and mix to fully distribute.

5. Put the sanding sugar in a small bowl.

6. Using your ice cream scoop, scoop out twenty-four equal-sized balls of dough and drop them onto the prepared cookie sheet.

7. Roll each ball between the palms of your hands and then roll them in the sanding sugar. Return the cookies to the tray and lightly press down on each one with the palm of your hand to slightly flatten the top.

8. Bake for 12 to 15 minutes, or until they are a lovely golden brown and firm to the touch.

9. Remove the cookies from the oven and allow them to cool on the cookie sheet.

You know the holidays have officially begun at Butter when the guys show up. With their little smiley faces and Smartie buttons, they act as the perfect ambassadors to welcome in the season (and when the stress of it all gets to be too much, you can chomp their heads off).

Gingerbread Guys

½ cup fancy molasses

⅓ cup dark brown sugar

⅓ cup granulated sugar

1 teaspoon ground cinnamon

1 teaspoon ground ginger

½ teaspoon baking soda

¾ cup butter, room temperature

2 eggs

3 ¾ cups all-purpose flour

FINISHING TOUCHES

1 recipe Royal Icing (page 122)

36 Smarties or M&M's (not counting
   the ones you will eat)

½ cup multicolored sprinkles (for
   their little hands and feet!)

MAKES: 1 ½ dozen (5-inch) gingerbread guys

YOU WILL NEED: 2 (11- x 17-inch)
rimmed cookie sheets lined with
parchment paper, 5-inch
gingerbread man cookie cutter,
8-inch piping bag fitted with a
small plain tip

STORAGE: These cookies will keep
in an airtight container for up to
2 weeks.

1. Preheat the oven to 350°F.

2. In a double boiler over medium heat, or a heatproof bowl set over a pot of simmering water, combine and stir the molasses, both sugars, cinnamon and ginger. When the sugars have melted, add the baking soda and stir. When the mixture bubbles up, remove the pot from the heat and set aside.

3. Place the butter in the bowl of a stand mixer fitted with a paddle attachment. Slowly pour the warm molasses mixture over the butter. With the machine running on medium speed, mix until the butter has completely melted and the mixture has cooled slightly.

4. Add the eggs one at a time, beating well after each addition. Scrape down the sides of the bowl.

5. With the mixer running on low speed, slowly add the flour until it is fully combined.

6. Lift the dough from the bowl and place it on a well-floured work surface. Use a rolling pin to roll out the dough to about ¼ inch thick.

7. Use your gingerbread man cookie cutter (or a cutter of your choice) to cut out about eighteen large cookies. Carefully transfer the cookies to the prepared trays and place them about ½ inch apart. You will need to combine the scraps and reroll the dough several times to use it all up, but not to worry as this is a very sturdy dough that doesn't mind being handled.

8. Bake for approximately 10 minutes, or until the cookies are still slightly soft to the touch in the center. I prefer a softer gingerbread cookie, but if you like yours crunchy, then bake them a little while longer.

9. Transfer the cookies to wire racks and allow them to cool completely before decorating.

10. While the cookies cool, prepare the Royal Icing. Transfer the royal icing to the piping bag fitted with the plain tip and let the fun begin. At Butter we like to ice eyes and a big smile on our guys, then add a couple of squeezes of icing to hold his buttons in place and finish his hands and feet off with a little more icing and a dip in some multicolored sprinkles. But hey, don't let us tell you what to do. Just like those snowflakes that we hope are falling, no two guys have to be alike!

There are a lot of things you can store in your freezer, but a roll of icebox cookies is one of the handiest, second only to rolls of cash. If you can find a spare moment in the weeks leading up to Christmas, I encourage you to whip up a batch. It takes but a moment and you will then be well prepared for an impromptu cookie exchange, last-minute entertaining or just a serious need for a warm cookie. Rumor has it Santa is pretty keen on them too, so save a few for the big guy when he stops by on Christmas Eve.

Cranberry Pistachio Icebox Cookies

1 cup butter, room temperature

1 ½ cups granulated sugar

1 large egg

1 teaspoon pure vanilla

2 ½ cups all-purpose flour

1 teaspoon salt

½ cup dried cranberries

½ cup pistachios, lightly chopped

Zest of 1 lemon

1 cup pistachios

MAKES: **4 dozen cookies**

YOU WILL NEED: **parchment paper, food processor or blender, plastic bench scraper or ruler, 2 (11- x 17-inch) rimmed cookie sheets lined with parchment paper**

STORAGE: **The frozen, wrapped dough will keep in the freezer for up to 3 months. Once baked, the cookies will keep in an airtight container for up to 1 week.**

1. In a stand mixer fitted with a paddle attachment, cream the butter and sugar until light and fluffy. Scrape down the sides of the bowl. Add the egg and vanilla and beat again until well combined. Scrape down the sides of the bowl.

2. With the mixer running on low speed, slowly add the flour and salt and mix until fully combined. Scrape down the sides of the bowl.

3. Add the cranberries, ½ cup chopped pistachios and lemon zest and mix until well combined.

4. Place half the dough on a large piece of parchment. Loosely shape the dough into a log. Pull the piece of parchment over the top of the log. Using your plastic bench scraper or ruler, push back on the parchment against the base of the log. This will help pack the dough tightly into a nice, even log.

5. In a food processor or blender, grind the 1 cup pistachios until quite fine. Unwrap your first log of dough and sprinkle half of the ground pistachios on the parchment paper. Roll the log across the pistachios to evenly coat all sides.

You can also roll the cookie logs in coarse sanding sugar instead of ground pistachios for an equally pretty but more cost-effective decoration.

6. Roll the parchment around the finished log and then wrap it tightly in plastic wrap. Repeat the process with the other half of the dough.

7. Place the rolled dough in the freezer for at least 2 hours, or overnight.

8. Preheat the oven to 350°F.

9. Slice each frozen log into twenty-four equal pieces and place the slices on the prepared trays. Bake for 12 to 15 minutes, or until lightly golden brown around the edges.

This dough is a nice base for lots of flavor options, so have some fun with it. One idea is to swap out the pistachios for pecans and the lemon zest for orange zest, but I leave it to you. I'm confident you will make some delicious choices.

We don't make a lot of bread at Butter, but panettone is one Christmas tradition that I insist on. It is a wonderful Italian bread studded with fruit and citrus zest. It is delicious all on its own or slathered in butter, but try using it for French toast on Christmas morning if you really want a treat. I love to give beautifully wrapped panettone and a bottle of pure maple syrup as a host gift when I'm invited to holiday parties. I'll include a little recipe for French toast with the stipulation that they must give me 30 minutes' notice prior to serving so I can hightail it over and join them.

Christmas Panettone

3 ½ cups all-purpose flour

2 packages instant yeast

½ teaspoon salt

½ cup whole milk

¼ cup water

⅓ cup butter

⅓ cup granulated sugar

2 large eggs

2 egg yolks

½ teaspoon pure vanilla

½ cup dried cranberries

½ cup golden raisins

½ cup dried sour cherries

½ cup candied citrus peel

Zest of 1 orange

Zest of 1 lemon

FINISHING TOUCHES

1 large egg

2 tablespoons heavy cream

MAKES: 1 large panettone

1. In a stand mixer fitted with a dough hook or paddle attachment, place the flour, yeast and salt. Set aside.

2. Place the milk and water in a medium pot over medium heat and add the butter and sugar. Stir until the milk is warm, but not boiling, and the butter has melted.

3. Add the warm milk mixture to the dry ingredients and mix on low speed until incorporated. Add the eggs, egg yolks and vanilla and continue to mix for 2 to 3 minutes.

4. Add the dried fruit, peel and citrus zests and mix for another 2 to 5 minutes. The dough will be quite soft and sticky.

5. Lightly butter or oil a large bowl and place the dough in it. Cover the bowl with a sheet of plastic wrap and place it in a warm, draft-free spot. Allow the dough to rise until it has doubled in size, about 90 minutes.

6. Once the dough has fully risen, remove the plastic wrap and punch the dough down in the bowl to release the air produced by the yeast. Turn the dough out onto a lightly floured board and allow it to rest for 10 minutes.

7. Shape the dough into a large ball by rolling it around in circles on the board with both hands. Place the ball of dough in your panettone pan or paper mold. Cover it loosely with a sheet of plastic wrap that has been lightly buttered on the underside. Place the pan on a cookie sheet in a warm, draft-free spot and

YOU WILL NEED: 1 (7- x 4-inch) panettone pan or a disposable paper panettone mold (available at most baking supply stores or online), pastry brush

STORAGE: Panettone can be kept in an airtight container or wrapped tightly for up to 1 week or in the freezer for up to 1 month.

Extra egg whites and egg yolks can be successfully saved for up to 2 days in your refrigerator. Make sure they are tightly covered with plastic wrap. Egg yolks tend to dry out so cover them in a thin layer of water before covering and remember to pour it off before use. At the bakery, we write the number of egg yolks or egg whites in the container on top of the plastic wrap they are covered in to remind us of exactly what we have on hand.

allow the dough to rise until it has doubled in size again and risen in a nice dome above the pan edges. Remove the plastic wrap.

8. Preheat the oven to 350°F. You will want to remove the top rack from the oven so you have ample room for the panettone.

9. In a small bowl, whisk together the egg and cream to create an egg wash for the top of the loaf. Use a pastry brush to gently coat the top of the panettone with it.

10. Bake for 30 minutes, or until the panettone is a lovely golden brown on top. A wooden skewer inserted in the middle should come out clean.

11. Allow the panettone to cool completely in the pan before removing and slicing or packaging.

*W*ith the constant fear of global warming upon us and the concern for what that would mean to the future of snowball fights, I decided to create a confection that would be both delicious and useful in desperate times.

Snowballs

2 cups granulated sugar

1 cup heavy cream

¼ cup plus 2 tablespoons butter

1 teaspoon pure vanilla

2 cups dark chocolate chips

2 cups unsweetened shredded
coconut

MAKES: **About 1 dozen (1-inch) balls**

YOU WILL NEED: **candy thermometer, 1 (9- x 9-inch) baking pan, buttered, 1 (11- x 17-inch) rimmed cookie sheet lined with parchment paper, small ice cream scoop**

STORAGE: **These balls will keep in an airtight container in the refrigerator for several weeks or in the freezer for up to 3 months.**

1. In a medium pot over high heat, add the sugar and cream and bring to a boil.

2. Once the cream mixture has reached a boil, add ¼ cup of the butter. Clip the candy thermometer to the side of the pot and turn down the heat so the mixture is at a low boil. Without stirring, maintain the boil until the candy thermometer reaches 240°F. Remove from the heat.

3. Gently stir in the vanilla and then carefully pour the cream mixture into the prepared baking pan. Set aside until it is loosely set and just warm to the touch, about 15 minutes.

4. Transfer the cream mixture to the bowl of a stand mixer fitted with a paddle attachment. Beat on high speed for 15 to 20 minutes, until light and fluffy. The cream mixture is very shiny and slippery when it first goes into the bowl and appears as though it will never get light and fluffy, but hang in there! In the last 5 minutes of the whip it transforms itself from a taffy-like confection to a light and fluffy nougat. Trust me!

5. Using a small ice cream scoop or two little spoons, roll the cream mixture into approximately twenty-four 1-inch balls of nougat and place them on the prepared cookie sheet. Place the sheet in the refrigerator while you are preparing the chocolate for coating.

6. In a double boiler over medium heat, or a small heatproof bowl placed over a pot of simmering water, melt the chocolate chips with the remaining 2 tablespoons butter over medium heat until smooth and shiny. Remove from the heat. ☞

7. Place the coconut in a medium bowl.

8. Dip each ball of nougat into the melted chocolate. Using a fork, roll it around to coat the whole surface. Use the fork to gently lift the ball from the chocolate (I sit it on top of the tines to lift it out rather than spear it) and then lightly tap it on the side of the bowl to remove any excess chocolate. You may need to rewarm the chocolate if it starts to thicken up as it cools.

9. Drop the chocolate-covered balls one at a time into the coconut and roll them around until completely coated. Place the finished snowballs back on the cookie sheet. Once you have completed all of them, put the tray back in the refrigerator for 10 to 15 minutes to help the chocolate set up.

Candy making is not for the faint of heart. It can be a bit finicky, but if you watch your candy thermometer carefully and follow these added instructions, all should work out delicious in the end.

Snowballs require you to bring the sugar syrup to a temperature of 240°F, also known as "soft-ball stage." That means that when you drop a bit of the boiled syrup into a glass of cool water, it will form a soft ball. When you lift the little ball from the water and place it on the palm of your hand, it will start to flatten after a few moments. For the best results, it is a good idea to use your candy thermometer and this cold water test.

I wonder how many people will get to this page, squish their face up and mutter "Blech" under their breath. Okay, that's fine. If that's the way you want to be, so be it. But if you are like me and consider fruitcake to be one of the many highlights of the holiday season, then I encourage you to read on. The rest of you should just grow up.

Butter's Delicious Fruitcake (Scout's honor)

2 cups raisins

½ cup dried figs, chopped

¾ cup dried sour cherries

½ cup dried cranberries

½ cup dried apricots, chopped

1 cup brandy

¾ cup honey

1 ½ cups all-purpose flour

1 teaspoon salt

1 teaspoon ground ginger

1 teaspoon ground cinnamon

¼ teaspoon ground cloves

1 cup pecans, chopped

1 cup butter, room temperature

¾ cup granulated sugar

4 large eggs

8 dried apricots, whole

8 pecans, whole

2 dried figs, halved

½ cup apricot jam

2 tablespoons water

1. Place the raisins, chopped figs, sour cherries, cranberries and chopped apricots in a large nonreactive bowl (glass or ceramic but not metal). Add the brandy and honey and stir to combine. Cover the bowl with plastic wrap and allow it to sit at room temperature for at least 24 hours or up to 1 week. We want the fruit soaking up all that lovely brandy.

2. Preheat the oven to 350°F.

3. In a large bowl, sift together the flour, salt, ginger, cinnamon and cloves. Stir in the chopped pecans and set aside.

4. In a stand mixer fitted with a paddle attachment, cream the butter and sugar on medium-high speed until light and fluffy. Scrape down the sides of the bowl.

5. Add the eggs one at a time, beating well after each addition. Scrape down the sides of the bowl again.

6. Fold in the dry ingredients and the fruit and brandy mixture.

7. Divide the batter between the two prepared pans, or two pretty paper pans, and smooth the tops over with the back of a spoon or a small offset spatula.

8. Bake for 50 to 60 minutes, or until the fruitcake is firm to the touch and a wooden skewer inserted in the center of a cake comes out clean.

9. Remove the cakes from the oven and allow them to cool slightly before removing from the pans for decorating and glazing. If you have baked the fruitcake in paper molds, you can simply move straight to the decorating and glazing. ☞

MAKES: **2 (8-inch) fruitcakes, 8 to 10 slices each**

YOU WILL NEED: **2 (8-inch) loaf pans, buttered (or 2 pretty paper loaf pans)**

The fruitcakes will keep in the refrigerator until the end of time if wrapped well in plastic wrap. Okay . . . not that long, but 1 month for sure!

10. Arrange the whole apricots, pecans and fig halves in a pretty pattern on top of each fruitcake There isn't a rule for this, so have some fun with it. It is just a nice way to indicate what yummy bits are tucked inside.

11. In a small pot, combine the apricot jam and water and bring them to a boil over medium heat. Remove from the heat. Using a pastry brush, coat the top of the fruitcakes and the decorative fruit with the apricot glaze. This will create an attractive and delicious sheen for the cakes and further seal in all that goodness. Allow the cakes to cool completely before slicing. I find that fruitcake slices even better if you use a serrated knife.

I love taking the classics we make at Butter every day and giving them a little holiday makeover. It's like buying these bars a new party dress for the festive season. Better not catch them under the mistletoe with a Gingerbread Guy (page 206)!

Peppermint Nanaimo Bars

BASE

2 cups graham crumbs

1 cup unsweetened shredded coconut

½ cup butter

¼ cup granulated sugar

¼ cup dark cocoa

1 large egg

1 teaspoon pure vanilla

FILLING

½ cup butter, room temperature

2 cups icing sugar

2 tablespoons heavy cream

1 teaspoon mint extract

1 to 2 drops red food coloring

TOPPING

¾ cup dark chocolate chips

2 tablespoons butter

2 to 3 candy canes

MAKES: 16 bars

YOU WILL NEED: 1 (9- x 9-inch) baking pan, buttered and lined with parchment paper, plastic resealable bag, rolling pin

1. For the base, in a large bowl, combine the graham crumbs and coconut.

2. In a medium pot over medium heat, warm ½ cup butter with the sugar and cocoa until the butter is melted and the sugar has dissolved. Remove from the heat. Allow to cool for a couple of minutes and then add the egg and vanilla and whisk to combine.

3. Pour the melted mixture over the graham crumb mixture and stir until well combined. Press into the prepared pan firmly and evenly. Set aside.

4. For the filling, in a stand mixer fitted with a paddle attachment, cream the butter and icing sugar on medium speed until pale. Scrape down the sides of the bowl and add the cream, mint extract and food coloring. Resume mixing on low speed until the food coloring has been dispersed so it doesn't spatter back at you and then turn the mixer speed to medium and mix until the filling is light and fluffy.

5. Use a small offset spatula to spread the filling across the top of the graham crumb base smoothly and evenly. Set aside.

6. For the topping, in a double boiler over medium heat, or a heatproof bowl set over a pot of simmering water, melt the chocolate chips and 2 tablespoons butter. Pour over the filling and spread it evenly with the back of a spoon or the small offset spatula. Tap the pan on the countertop to help smooth the chocolate layer. Set aside.

7. Place the candy canes in a small resealable plastic bag, seal the bag and give it a few good whacks with a rolling pin to crush the candy canes. Sprinkle the candy cane bits over the chocolate layer.

8. Place the pan in the refrigerator for at least 1 hour, or until the chocolate topping has set.

9. Run a small knife along the sides of the pan that do not have parchment and then carefully remove the slab from the pan. Cut the slab into sixteen bars. Make sure to use at least a 10-inch knife to avoid cutting and dragging the knife across the bars. It is also helpful to wipe the blade between cuts to ensure a clean cut.

*M*incemeat can be one of those things that really divides a room, and to some degree I can understand why. Its flavor can be a little intense for some. In an effort to create harmony at this special time of year I came up with this bar, added a smidge of brandy (my secret harmony enhancer) and finished with a dusting of freshly fallen icing sugar. Are you starting to think you might like to join me on this side of the room?

Mince Harmony Bars

2 ½ cups all-purpose flour

1 teaspoon baking powder

½ teaspoon salt

¾ cup butter, room temperature

1 ½ cups dark brown sugar

2 large eggs

2 tablespoons brandy

1 teaspoon pure vanilla

¾ cup good quality mincemeat

FINISHING TOUCHES

Icing sugar for dusting, approximately 2 tablespoons

MAKES: 16 bars

YOU WILL NEED: 1 (9- x 9-inch) baking pan, buttered and lined with parchment paper, small sieve for dusting icing sugar

STORAGE: These bars will keep in an airtight container for up to 1 week or in the freezer for up to 3 months.

1. Preheat the oven to 350°F.

2. On a large piece of parchment paper, sift the flour, baking powder and salt. Set aside.

3. In a stand mixer fitted with a paddle attachment, cream the butter and sugar until light and fluffy. Scrape down the sides of the bowl.

4. Add the eggs one at a time, beating well after each addition. Scrape down the sides of the bowl. Add the brandy and vanilla and beat again.

5. With the mixer running on low speed, slowly add the dry ingredients. Mix until just combined. Add the mincemeat and mix again until fully incorporated.

6. Place the dough in the prepared pan and spread the top smooth with a small offset spatula.

7. Bake for 30 to 35 minutes, or until a wooden skewer inserted in the center of the slab comes out clean.

8. Remove the slab from the oven and allow it to cool in the pan. Once the slab has cooled, lift it from the pan using the parchment handles.

9. Place the icing sugar in a small sieve and lightly dust the top of the slab. It can now be cut into sixteen bars. Make sure to use at least a 10-inch knife to avoid cutting and dragging the knife across the bars. It is also helpful to wipe the blade between cuts to ensure a clean cut.

*I*t was on a warm June day that I set out to create this recipe and soon discovered that eggnog was not readily available in any grocery store. Go figure. Well, I wouldn't let a little thing like that stop me, so I forged ahead. The result was fantastic, if I do say so myself. Eggnog, who needs ya?

Eggnog-less Bars

BASE

2 cups graham crumbs

1 teaspoon ground allspice

½ cup butter, melted and cooled

FILLING

Two 8-ounce packages cream
   cheese, full fat

300 mL can condensed milk

1 large egg

¼ cup all-purpose flour

2 tablespoons brandy

½ teaspoon ground nutmeg, plus a
   little extra for sprinkling

MAKES: 16 bars

YOU WILL NEED: 1 (9- x 9-inch)
   baking pan, buttered and lined
   with parchment paper

STORAGE: These bars will keep in
   an airtight container for up to
   1 week or in the freezer for up
   to 3 months.

1. Preheat the oven to 350°F.

2. For the base, in a medium bowl, use a spatula or large spoon to combine the graham crumbs, allspice and butter.

3. Press the mixture firmly and evenly into the prepared pan. Bake for 10 minutes, or until a light golden brown. Remove from the oven and set aside. Leave the oven on.

4. For the filling, in a stand mixer fitted with a paddle attachment, cream the cream cheese on medium speed until light and fluffy. Scrape down the sides of the bowl and add the condensed milk, egg, flour, brandy and nutmeg. Continue to mix until well combined.

5. Pour the cream cheese mixture over the baked graham base, use a small offset spatula to spread it evenly and sprinkle more nutmeg over top.

6. Bake for 20 minutes, or until the center is firm.

7. Remove the slab from the oven and allow it to cool completely in the pan or place in the refrigerator overnight.

8. Run a small knife along the two edges of the pan that do not have parchment. Carefully remove the slab from the pan and cut it into sixteen bars. Make sure to use at least a 10-inch knife to avoid cutting and dragging the knife across the bars. It is also helpful to wipe the blade between cuts to ensure a clean cut.

This is a simple but delicious cake that leaves the whole house smelling like Christmas. It would be perfect to nibble on while tucked up on the sofa watching *It's a Wonderful Life*. I'm sorry, did I just hear you say, "What is *It's a Wonderful Life*?" Only the best darn Christmas movie ever made, that's what! Report back after you've seen it and then maybe I'll let you have some cake. Just maybe.

Orange Gingerbread Cake

2 ¼ cups all-purpose flour

1 ½ teaspoons baking soda

2 teaspoons ground ginger

½ teaspoon ground cinnamon

¼ teaspoon ground cloves

½ teaspoon salt

¾ cup vegetable oil

⅔ cup fancy molasses

⅔ cup dark brown sugar

1 large egg

1 tablespoon freshly grated ginger

Zest of 1 orange

1 ½ cups boiling water

ORANGE GLAZE

2 cups icing sugar, sifted

Zest of 1 orange

3 to 4 tablespoons hot water

MAKES: **1 Bundt cake, 10 to 12 slices**

YOU WILL NEED: **1 (6-cup) Bundt pan, buttered and floured, 1 (11- x 17-inch) rimmed cookie sheet (optional)**

1. Preheat the oven to 350°F.

2. On a large piece of parchment paper, sift the flour, baking soda, ground ginger, cinnamon, cloves and salt. Set aside.

3. In a stand mixer fitted with a paddle attachment, combine the oil, molasses, brown sugar and egg. Mix on medium-high speed until well combined.

4. Turn the mixer speed to low and slowly add the dry ingredients. Scrape down the sides of the bowl and add the grated ginger and orange zest. Mix to combine.

5. With the mixer still on low speed, slowly add the boiling water and mix until fully combined.

6. Pour the batter into the prepared pan and bake for 40 to 45 minutes, or until a wooden skewer inserted in the center of the cake comes out clean.

7. Remove the cake from the oven and allow it to cool in the pan for about 10 minutes, then transfer to a wire rack to cool completely. Place the wire rack on top of a cookie sheet (to catch any drips while glazing).

8. In a medium bowl, whisk the icing sugar and zest with the hot water to make a thick, shiny glaze.

9. When the cake has cooled completely, carefully spoon the glaze on the top of the cake and watch it slowly drizzle down the sides. Yum. Allow the glaze to set for about 30 minutes at room temperature before serving.

hese cookies couldn't be easier or more delicious. I am not sure why I insist on only making them during the month of December other than to prevent myself from eating them all year long!

Pecan Crescents

1 cup pecans, chopped

1 cup butter, room temperature

1 ¼ cups granulated sugar

1 ½ teaspoons pure vanilla

2 cups all-purpose flour

½ teaspoon salt

MAKES: **2 dozen crescents**

YOU WILL NEED: **2 (11- x 17-inch) rimmed cookie sheets lined with parchment paper**

STORAGE: **These cookies will keep in an airtight container for up to 2 weeks or in the freezer for up to 3 months.**

1. Preheat the oven to 350°F.

2. Place the pecans on one of the prepared cookie sheets and bake for approximately 10 minutes, or until lightly toasted. Make sure to stir the nuts at the halfway point to ensure even toasting. Remove the nuts from the oven and allow them to cool in the pan before giving them a light chop. Set aside. Leave the oven on.

3. In a stand mixer fitted with a paddle attachment, cream the butter with ¾ cup of the sugar until light and fluffy. Scrape down the sides of the bowl. Add the vanilla and beat again.

4. Turn the mixer speed to low and slowly add the flour, salt and pecans while the machine is running. Turn the mixer speed to medium and continue to mix until the dough pulls together.

5. Place the remaining ½ cup sugar in a small bowl. Divide the dough into twenty-four equal pieces and then shape each piece into a crescent shape, approximately 2 inches long. Place each cookie in the bowl of sugar and carefully coat it on all sides. Once coated, place the cookies on the prepared cookie sheets, about 1 inch apart.

6. Bake for 12 to 15 minutes, or until the cookies are a lovely golden brown around the edges.

7. Remove from the oven and allow the cookies to cool slightly on the baking sheets before transferring them to wire racks to cool completely.

*W*ondering what to give as teacher gifts this holiday? No worries. Butter's got your back. These smooth and creamy caramels with just a hint of sea salt make a perfect little gift once you wrap them up in parchment and tuck them in a cellophane bag. Finish it off with a pretty red ribbon and you are good to go. See? No worries.

Butter's Salted Caramels

2 cups heavy cream

¼ cup butter

1 teaspoon salt

½ cup light corn syrup

¼ cup water

1 ½ cups granulated sugar

¾ cup dark brown sugar

1 teaspoon pure vanilla

1 tablespoon sea salt for sprinkling

MAKES: **4 dozen pieces or 8 bags of 6 (depending on how much quality-control tasting you do)**

YOU WILL NEED: **1 (9- x 13-inch) baking pan, buttered and lined with parchment paper, candy thermometer, 48 sheets of parchment paper cut into 2- x 3-inch pieces**

STORAGE: **Once packaged, the caramels will keep for up to 1 month.**

1. In a medium pot over low heat, combine the cream, butter and salt. Stir until the butter has melted, then remove from the heat and set aside.

2. In a medium stockpot (about 5 inches deep), combine the corn syrup and water with both sugars. Stir to form a grainy paste. Clip your candy thermometer to the side of the pot and turn the heat to medium-high. Allow the temperature to reach 280°F. Do not stir the mixture.

3. When the sugar mixture has reached 280°F, remove the pan from the heat and slowly whisk in the warm cream mixture. It will bubble up, but fear not. This is why I asked you to use a deep pot.

4. Return the pot to medium-high heat and, without stirring, allow the mixture to reach 250°F.

5. Remove from the heat and gently stir in the vanilla.

6. Carefully pour the hot caramel into the prepared baking pan and use a spatula to scrape down the sides of the pot and spread the caramel evenly across the pan.

7. Sprinkle the top of the caramels evenly with the sea salt and then set the pan aside to cool at room temperature for at least 2 hours or even overnight.

8. Run a small knife along the edges of the pan that are not covered by parchment and then carefully lift the slab of caramel from the pan. Using a large knife, cut the caramels into forty-eight evenly sized pieces and then wrap each caramel in a piece of parchment and twist the ends to close tightly.

I like to think of myself as a bit of a spicy nut, but that's another story. We make buckets of these nuts during the holiday season at Butter, package them up in cello bags and line our shelves. They are the perfect little snack to put out before dinner when entertaining, and if you are willing to share, they make a lovely gift.

Butter's Spicy Nuts

2 egg whites

½ cup light brown sugar

1 teaspoon salt

¼ cup melted butter, cooled

2 teaspoons smoked paprika

1 teaspoon smoked chilli powder

4 cups mixed nuts (Pecans, cashews, almonds, hazelnuts or walnuts. Some of each or all one kind. Your choice.)

MAKES: **4 cups nuts**

YOU WILL NEED: **1 (11- x 17-inch) rimmed cookie sheet lined with parchment paper**

STORAGE: **These nuts will keep in an airtight container for up to 2 weeks.**

1. Preheat the oven to 350°F.

2. In a stand mixer fitted with a whisk attachment, whip the egg whites until frothy. (See page 18.) Add the brown sugar and salt and continue to whip until the whites are quite stiff.

3. Remove the bowl from the mixer and gently fold in the cooled, melted butter and spices. Then fold in the nuts, making sure to evenly coat them all.

4. Pour the nuts onto the prepared cookie sheet and use a spatula to spread them in an even layer.

5. Bake the nuts for 20 minutes. Remove the nuts from the oven and use the spatula to turn them over and mix them up a little.

6. Return the nuts to the oven and bake for another 15 minutes, or until they are a lovely deep brown.

7. Remove the nuts from the oven and allow them to cool completely on the cookie sheet before using your hands to break up any clusters that may have formed.

*S*ome may call these little gems rum balls, but at Butter they are better known as Yum Balls! They are the perfect addition to a holiday baking platter, or a nice little shot to your system before you head out to tackle the holiday shopping. I use Nabisco Nilla Wafers for this recipe.

Yum Balls

1 cup dark chocolate chips

⅔ cup sour cream, full fat

⅓ cup almond paste

3 cups vanilla wafer cookies, ground (approximately one box)

2 cups chocolate crumbs

2 cups icing sugar

⅓ cup dark cocoa

⅔ cup white rum

½ cup butter, melted

2 cups chocolate sprinkles

MAKES: **4 dozen balls**

YOU WILL NEED: **food processor or blender, small ice cream scoop, 1 (11- x 17-inch) rimmed cookie sheet lined with parchment paper**

STORAGE: **You can transfer the finished balls to an airtight container lined with parchment paper and store in the refrigerator for up to 1 month or in the freezer for up to 3 months.**

1. In a double boiler over medium heat, or a small heatproof bowl placed over a pot of simmering water, melt the chocolate chips. Remove from the heat.

2. In a stand mixer fitted with a paddle attachment, combine the melted chocolate with the sour cream and almond paste and mix on medium speed until well combined.

3. Empty the box of vanilla wafers into the food processor or blender and blend on high until the wafers are finely ground.

4. In a large bowl, combine the ground wafers, chocolate crumbs, icing sugar, cocoa, rum and melted butter. Stir with a large spoon or spatula until well combined and then add to the ingredients in the mixer.

5. Turn the mixer speed to medium and mix until everything has pulled together nicely to form a dark and delicious paste, scraping down the sides of the bowl at least once during the mixing process.

6. Refrigerate the dough in the mixer bowl for at least 1 hour or even overnight.

7. Using a small ice cream scoop, drop the balls onto the prepared cookie sheet. Place the chocolate sprinkles in a bowl large enough that you can get both your hands into it, to avoid sprinkles flying all around the kitchen. Roll each ball between your palms until smooth and then drop it into the chocolate sprinkles. Scoop up some sprinkles in each hand and press them around a ball and roll it again to fully coat.

This is the only holiday that we don't celebrate together at Butter. Never have. Why? Well, simply because we aren't there. It has been a Butter tradition since the very beginning to close the shop for two weeks at the end of the year. We make it all the way to December 24, bleary-eyed, exhausted but still smiling and slightly giddy. When 4 o'clock arrives, we lock the doors. The bakery erupts in cheers and high-fives for all the work that lies behind us and the vacation that stretches ahead. We line the work tables with any extra baking and invite everyone who works for Butter to fill boxes to enjoy over the holidays with family and friends. We hug, we kiss and we wish each other well. We'll meet again in the New Year, rested, re-energized and ready to start baking.

*M*y New Year's resolution is to keep thinking up more ways to include cupcakes in holiday celebrations. I think I am off to an excellent start.

Champagne Cupcakes

1 ½ cups all-purpose flour

1 teaspoon baking powder

½ teaspoon baking soda

½ teaspoon salt

½ cup butter, room temperature

1 cup granulated sugar

2 large eggs

½ cup champagne

½ cup buttermilk

½ teaspoon pure vanilla

CHAMPAGNE SYRUP

¼ cup granulated sugar

¼ cup water

¼ cup champagne

FINISHING TOUCHES

1 recipe Champagne Butter Cream
    (page 121)

Silver flakes (optional)

MAKES: 1 dozen cupcakes

YOU WILL NEED: muffin pan lined
    with paper liners, large ice
    cream scoop, wooden skewer,
    14-inch piping bag fitted with a
    large star tip

1. Preheat the oven to 350°F.

2. On a large piece of parchment paper, sift the flour, baking powder, baking soda and salt. Set aside.

3. In a stand mixer fitted with a paddle attachment, cream the butter and sugar on high speed until light and fluffy. Scrape down the sides of the bowl.

4. Add the eggs one at a time, beating well after each addition. Scrape down the sides of the bowl.

5. Measure out the champagne. Make sure to let the bubbles settle so you get an accurate measure. In a bowl, whisk together the champagne, buttermilk and vanilla.

6. Turn the mixer speed to low and add the dry ingredients in three parts, alternating with the liquid ingredients in two parts, and beginning and ending with the dry. Scrape down the sides of the bowl several times during this process to make sure everything is fully combined.

7. Use the ice cream scoop to fill each paper liner about three-quarters full with batter.

8. Bake for 15 to 20 minutes, or until a wooden skewer inserted in the center of a cupcake comes out clean.

9. Meanwhile, prepare the Champagne Syrup for drenching the cupcakes. In a small pot over high heat, combine the sugar and water. Without stirring, allow the sugar to come to a boil. Allow to boil for about 2 minutes, making sure all the sugar has dissolved. Remove from the heat and allow the syrup to cool for several minutes before whisking in the champagne. Set aside.

10. Remove the cupcakes from the oven and allow them to cool in the pan for about 5 minutes before transferring them to a wire rack. Use a wooden skewer to poke several holes in the top of each warm cupcake. Use a pastry brush to drench the top of each cupcake with the Champagne Syrup. Allow the cupcakes to cool completely while you prepare the Champagne Butter Cream.

11. Fill your 14-inch piping bag fitted with a large star tip with Champagne Butter Cream and pipe it over the top of each cupcake. You can finish with a sprinkle of silver flakes to add a little more sparkle. After all, New Year's is all about the sparkle.

he perfect little treat alongside a glass or two of champagne, the night before or the morning after, will set you up nicely to face the year ahead.

Boozy Chocolate Truffles

1 ½ cups dark chocolate chips

2 tablespoons butter

¾ cup heavy cream

2 tablespoons brandy

¼ cup dark cocoa

MAKES: 2 dozen truffles

YOU WILL NEED: 1 (11- x 17-inch) rimmed cookie sheet lined with parchment paper, melon baller or small ice cream scoop

STORAGE: These truffles will keep nicely in the refrigerator for up to 1 week or in the freezer for up to 3 months.

1. Place the chocolate chips and butter in a medium bowl. Set aside.

2. In a small pot set over medium heat, warm the cream until it starts to boil. Remove from the heat.

3. Pour the hot cream over the chocolate and butter. Allow it to sit for several minutes and then whisk until the chocolate and butter are melted and smooth.

4. Place the bowl in the refrigerator for at least 1 hour to allow the chocolate to set.

5. When the chocolate has set, use your melon baller or ice cream scoop to scoop and drop the truffles onto the prepared cookie sheet.

6. Fill a shallow bowl with the cocoa. Roll each ball quickly between the palms of your hands and then roll in the cocoa to lightly coat. Place the ball back on the cookie sheet and repeat with the rest of the truffles.

7. Place the truffles in the refrigerator to help them firm up, as the heat of your hands from rolling them will have softened the chocolate.

Chocolate truffles are a little like butter cream: a vehicle for flavors.
Consider changing up the liquor and the coating to create different options.

Crushed pecans	Peppermint schnapps	Cherry brandy	Amaretto
Bourbon	Chocolate sprinkles	Fine unsweetened coconut	Toasted almonds, finely chopped

T set out to create this dessert based on one Paul and I used to buy at a little neighborhood spot some twenty-five years ago. It was a big treat for us back then, saved for special occasions, and we were more than a little sad when the creators of this decadence closed up shop and cut off our supply. All these years later I have finally rectified the situation and New Year's seems like the perfect time to indulge.

Triple Chocolate Mousse with Coffee Crème Anglaise

1 ½ cups heavy cream

DARK CHOCOLATE LAYER

½ cup dark chocolate chips

3 egg yolks

1 large egg

¼ cup sugar

MILK CHOCOLATE LAYER

2 tablespoons heavy cream

1 teaspoon gelatin

½ cup milk chocolate chips

3 egg yolks

1 large egg

¼ cup sugar

WHITE CHOCOLATE LAYER

2 tablespoons heavy cream

1 teaspoon gelatin

½ cup white chocolate chips

3 egg yolks

1 large egg

¼ cup sugar

FINISHING TOUCHES

1 recipe Coffee Crème Anglaise
   (page 243)

1. In a stand mixer fitted with a whisk attachment, whip 1 ½ cups of cream until soft peaks form. Set aside.

2. For the dark chocolate layer, in a double boiler over medium heat, or a small heatproof bowl set over simmering water, melt the dark chocolate chips.

3. In a small bowl, whisk together the egg yolks, egg and sugar. Add to the chocolate and continue whisking until the chocolate starts to thicken. Remove from the heat and allow to cool for approximately 5 minutes. Gently fold in one-third of the whipped cream.

4. Fill your 14-inch piping bag fitted with a large plain tip with the dark chocolate mousse and carefully divide it between the six glasses to create your bottom layer. Place the glasses in the refrigerator while you make the next layer.

5. For the milk chocolate layer, place the 2 tablespoons cream in a small pot set over medium heat until just warm (you can also do this in your microwave for about 15 seconds). Remove the pot from the heat and pour the cream into a small bowl. Sprinkle the gelatin over the top of the cream and allow it to sit for several minutes to give it time to soften and bloom. ☞

The dark chocolate layer doesn't need gelatin. Dark chocolate contains a high percentage of cocoa solids and no milk solids whereas milk chocolate and white chocolate contain little or no cocoa solids and varying degrees of milk solids, thus making it harder for them to set up in the same way the dark chocolate will.

MAKES: **6 servings**

YOU WILL NEED: **14-inch piping bag fitted with a plain tip, 6 pretty glasses (about 1 cup each)**

STORAGE: **The mousse will keep in the refrigerator for up to 3 days.**

6. Repeat steps 2 and 3 using the milk chocolate chips, making sure to whisk the softened gelatin and cream with the eggs and sugar and then carry on through step 4 to create the second layer.

7. Repeat steps 5 through 6 with the white chocolate to create the final layer.

8. Place the glasses back in the refrigerator and allow them to chill, uncovered, to set the gelatin for at least 2 hours, or overnight.

9. Prepare the Coffee Crème Anglaise.

10. To serve the mousse, spoon 2 to 3 tablespoons of the crème anglaise atop each one. It will work its way down the layers as your guests start to spoon up the mousse.

rème anglaise is a delicious custard sauce that is easy to make and even easier to enjoy. Consider using it beside a slice of chocolate cake or poured over a bowl of fruit crumble in place of whipped cream or a scoop of ice cream.

Crème Anglaise

1 vanilla bean

1 cup heavy cream

3 egg yolks

½ cup sugar

MAKES: **1 cup sauce**

YOU WILL NEED: **fine mesh sieve**

STORAGE: **This can be made 1 day ahead and will keep in the refrigerator for several days.**

1. Use a small paring knife to split the vanilla bean. Use the tip of the knife to scrape out the vanilla seeds and set them aside. You can place the empty vanilla bean in your vanilla bottle to further enhance the flavor, or tuck it inside your sugar jar to give the sugar a subtle vanilla flavor.

2. In a small pot, heat the cream over medium heat until bubbles just begin to form at the edges of the pot. Remove from the heat.

3. In a small bowl, whisk together the egg yolks, sugar and vanilla seeds.

4. Pour half of the warm cream into the egg yolks and whisk to combine. Pour the egg and cream mixture back into the pot with the remaining cream and whisk to combine.

5. Return the pot to medium heat and continue stirring until the crème anglaise thickens slightly and can coat the back of a spoon.

6. Remove from the heat. Pour the crème anglaise through a fine mesh sieve into a bowl. Cover with plastic wrap and place in the refrigerator to cool.

COFFEE CRÈME ANGLAISE

Add 1 tablespoon espresso powder with the cream

ORANGE CRÈME ANGLAISE

Add the zest of 1 orange + 1 tablespoon Cointreau (optional) with the cream

Sweet Packages

Baked goods are for sharing and it's a known fact that your baking tastes better when you share it with others. And who wouldn't want to be known as "That generous person with the great-tasting baked goods"? Little packages of sweet treats make for perfect teacher gifts, loot bags, a warm welcome or even a little something for everyone's place setting at your Thanksgiving table. Here I've put together some fun and inexpensive ways to package up your goodies, but let your imagination run wild and have some fun with it!

LITTLE PAPER BAGS OF ALL SHAPES AND SIZES

A stash of waxed sandwich bags is always a good thing to have on hand. We use droves of simple white ones at the bakery every day but they are readily available in craft shops and paper goods stores in a wide range of colors and patterns. A small pink bag of Little Cinnamon Heart Cookies (page 24) sealed with a tiny clothes peg makes for a perfect Valentine gift, and a few Lil' Ghost Meringues (page 167) peeking out of a bag that's been stamped with the word "BOO!" would make for pretty cute Halloween handouts.

HELLO, CELLO!

I couldn't possibly tell you how many cello bags we have used at Butter over the last eight years. We use them for everything from our marshmallows to loaves, right down to Zelda's favorite dog cookies (page 148). Our shelves are lined with crisp cello bags filled with baked goodness. Even the most basic of treats is elevated once packaged and tied with a lovely ribbon. It's such a simple thing but people always appreciate the special care and extra step you took. A tray of Little Meringue Booties (page 94) lined up in cello bags tied with pink or blue satin ribbon would make for the perfect little take-away should you even host a baby shower.

VINTAGE PLATES AND PLATTERS

Over the years, anytime I have spied an inexpensive but pretty little vintage plate or platter at a yard sale or flea market I have bought it up and tucked it away for future gifts of baking. Imagine the added beauty of the presentation when you bring someone Strawberry Cupcakes (page 84) on a pretty platter. Once they've eaten up all the cupcakes, the platter is theirs for the keeping. They can hold on to it or fill it with their own baking for someone else and carry on with the tradition. You might also want to consider a little stash of vintage teacups. They make the most lovely little vessel to tuck tiny treats like Snowballs (page 213) or Yum Balls (page 233) into. Should you also include a tin of tea, the teacup would prove very handy once all the goodies have been gobbled up.

MASON JAR, COOKIE JAR. WHAT'S THE DIFFERENCE?

My local dollar store is the greatest resource for a variety of containers that you can fill up with baking. Of all the things I have discovered there, I think the glass canning jars with a rubber seal are the greatest. I love to fill them up at Christmastime with Gingerbread Guys (page 206) or Pecan Crescents (page 227) and hang a little tag off the side that reads "Cookies for Santa." It makes for a perfect hostess gift. This idea would work anytime of year but make sure to switch up the Gingerbread Guys and hang tag or it might get confusing.

Some of my favorite containers to package baked goods in during the holiday season are bamboo steamers. Yet another item I discovered at the dollar store and cheap as chips to buy. They come in a variety of sizes and you can layer them up as high as you like. At Christmastime I will stack a steamer three layers high and fill each layer with a variety of baking. I will sometimes use paper muffin cup liners or parchment paper to hold or separate the different baking and then I tie the whole thing up with a wide satin ribbon and a couple of jingle bells or a piece of holly. If you were feeling really creative you could create a little guidebook with drawings and descriptions of each treat (just like the ones you find in a box of chocolates) and tuck it inside. Imagine the look of delight on your friends' and family's faces as they lift each layer to discover Snowballs (page 213), Eggnog-less Bars (page 222), Butter's Salted Caramels (page 228) and Yum Balls (page 233).

I hope you send me one. I'd really like that.

How to Tie the Perfect Bow

Mastering a good bow is a life skill that will take you far. We tie a lot of bows at Butter every day. And I mean a lot! It really is very easy once you figure it out. A couple of practice rounds and you will be wrapping anything and everything with big satin bows.

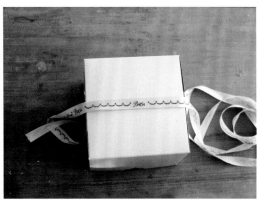

1. Let's pretend the top of the box needing to be wrapped is the face of a clock. Lay your piece of ribbon across the top of the box from the 3 to the 9, with about an 8-inch tail hanging off the 9 side. The rest of the length of the ribbon will be hanging off the 3 side.

2. Wrap the balance of the ribbon on the 3 side under the box and come up at the 9.

3. Cross the ribbon coming up from under the box over the top of the ribbon on the face of the box and head toward 12. Wrap the ribbon under the box again and bring it up at the 6.

4. Take the 8-inch tail in your left hand and lift it up to pull the first point where the ribbon crosses toward the center of the box. In your right hand, take the balance of the ribbon coming up from 6 and wrap it over (toward 11) and under the point where the ribbon crosses (toward 5). You should now have a nice little intersection where the ribbon from all four sides meets.

5. Take the lower ribbon in your right hand and make a loop.

6. Take the upper ribbon in your left hand and wrap it over and under the base the loop.

7. Pull the ribbon through the opening, which will create the second loop.

8. Pull tight to make a bow. Voila! You did it! Trim the ends of the ribbon with sharp scissors and there you have the perfect bow!

People to Celebrate!

To Mum and Dad. Thanks for giving me such happy childhood memories, full of celebration.

To Nonna. Thank you for all the cookies.

To Maggie, Trish, Naoe and Naomi, four of the most beautiful and talented women I know. Thank you for doing such a wonderful job. You make my crazy, chaotic life possible and for this I am truly grateful.

To Satomi, Justina, Kevin, Anawin, Noami, Aline and the rest of my Butter family. Thank you for all your hard work, dedication and laughter. You make getting up and coming to work everyday a total joy.

To my dear friends, the Buttersons, the Cartwrights and the Murphys. No celebration would feel complete without you.

To Stephanie Vogler of The Cross, Andrea Molnar of Baccis and Jessica Clark of Quince. Thank you for having such beautiful stores full of beautiful things. All your cake stands, platters, plates, flowers and table linens made my baked goods shine.

To Babette and her momma, Claire. Babette you are a star and your Momma has a nice front porch.

To Mo. Good hair can make even the worst day a party.

To Robert McCullough of Appetite. Thank you so much for making books with me, but more importantly, for your support and friendship. It means the world.

To Leslie Cameron, Bhavna Chauhan and Kelly Hill. I am so grateful for all your hard work, talent and kindness. Through it you have brought this book to life.

To Janis Donnaud. The best darn agent a girl could hope for. They say life can turn on a dime but for me it was your email. Thank you for looking after me.

To Janis Nicolay, the most talented photographer on the planet. How did I get so lucky? Working alongside you isn't work at all. It's a dream. Thank you so much for all that you do.

To Paul and India. Just having you next to me is reason enough to celebrate every day. Thank you for your unwavering support, love and laughter.

Index